THE ULTIMATE KETO DIET after 60

Kailyn Clark

© **Copyright 2024 - All rights reserved.**

The content contained within this book may not be reproduced, duplicated, or transmitted without direct written permission from the author or the publisher.

Under no circumstances will any blame or legal responsibility be held against the publisher, or author, for any damages, reparation, or monetary loss due to the information contained within this book, either directly or indirectly.

Legal Notice:

This book is copyright protected. It is only for personal use. You cannot amend, distribute, sell, use, quote, or paraphrase any part, or the content within this book, without the consent of the author or publisher.

Disclaimer Notice:

Please note the information contained within this document is for educational and entertainment purposes only. All effort has been executed to present accurate, up-to-date, reliable, complete information. No warranties of any kind are declared or implied. Readers acknowledge that the author is not engaged in the rendering of legal, financial, medical, or professional advice. The content within this book has been derived from various sources. Please consult a licensed professional before attempting any techniques outlined in this book.

By reading this document, the reader agrees that under no circumstances is the author responsible for any losses, direct or indirect, that are incurred as a result of the use of the information contained within this document, including, but not limited to, errors, omissions, or inaccuracies.

Table of contents

Introduction 7
Basics of the Keto Diet 8
Processes in the Body on the Keto Diet 10
Tips for Starting and Maintaining Ketosis 12
Measurement Conversion Tables 14
1. Breakfasts 15
    1.1 Omelet with Avocado and Cheese 15
    1.2 Scrambled Eggs with Bacon and Greens 15
    1.3 Almond Flour Pancakes 16
    1.4 Coconut Flour Waffles 16
    1.5 Chia Seed Porridge 17
    1.6 Scrambled Eggs with Salmon and Spinach 17
    1.7 Avocado Baked with Egg 18
    1.8 Avocado Cocoa Pudding 18
    1.7 Avocado Baked with Egg 19
    1.8 Avocado Cocoa Pudding 19
    1.9 Pancakes with Berries 20
    1.10 Frittata with Vegetables and Cheese 20
    1.11 Shakshuka with Sausages 21
    1.12 Granola with Coconut and Nuts 21
    1.13 Salad with Eggs and Avocado 22
    1.14 Spinach and Avocado Smoothie 22
2. Snacks and Light Meals 23
    2.1 Salmon and Avocado Rolls 23
    2.2 Tuna and Egg Salad 23
    2.3 Cauliflower Soup 24
    2.4 Chicken and Avocado Soup 24
    2.5 Chicken and Cheese Sandwich 25
    2.6 Bacon and Cheese Cupcakes 25
    2.7 Zucchini Fritters 26
    2.8 Caprese Salad with Avocado 26
    2.9 Cheese Sticks 27
    2.10 Lettuce Leaf Tacos 27
    2.11 Vegetable Omelet Roll 28
    2.12 Mushroom Cream Soup 28
    2.13 Lettuce Leaf Burgers 29
    2.14 Tomato and Basil Bruschetta 29
3. Main Dishes 30
    3.1 Baked Beef with Rosemary 30
    3.2 Almond Crust Pizza 30
    3.3 Chicken Breasts in Creamy Sauce 31
    3.4 Pork in Barbecue Sauce 31
    3.5 Grilled Salmon with Lemon and Dill 32
    3.6 Spaghetti with Meat Sauce 32
    3.7 Baked Cod with Broccoli 33
    3.8 Zucchini Lasagna 33

The Ultimate Keto Diet After 60

3.9 Beef Fajitas 34
3.10 Pork and Cabbage Stew 34
3.11 Chicken Curry 35
3.12 Beef Stew with Mushrooms 35
3.13 Chicken Fricassee with Vegetables 36
3.14 Turkey Kebab 36

4. Fish and Seafood 37
4.1 Salmon Fillet with Lemon Butter and Asparagus 37
4.2 Shrimp in Garlic Sauce 37
4.3 Baked Cod with Broccoli and Cheese 38
4.4 Sea Bass with Olives and Tomatoes 38
4.5 Grilled Tuna with Avocado 39
4.6 Squid and Cucumber Salad 39
4.7 Steamed Salmon with Green Beans 40
4.8 Fish Soup with Salmon 40
4.9 Shrimp Cocktail with Avocado 41
4.10 Baked Trout with Lemon and Herbs 41
4.11 Fish and Avocado Rolls 42
4.12 Crab Cakes with Tartar Sauce 42
4.13 Mussels in Cream Sauce 43
4.14 Fish and Avocado Ceviche 43

5. Meat and Poultry 44
5.1 Chicken Breasts with Broccoli and Cheese 44
5.2 Steak with Garlic Butter 44
5.3 Baked Chicken Wings in Spicy Sauce 45
5.4 Pork with Cauliflower 45
5.5 Turkey Meatballs with Avocado Sauce 46
5.6 Pan-Fried Duck with Orange Sauce 46
5.7 Chicken Curry with Coconut Milk 47
5.8 Garlic and Rosemary Baked Ribs 47
5.9 Beef with Mushrooms in Cream Sauce 48
5.10 Baked Turkey with Brussels Sprouts 48
5.11 Chicken Skewers with Green Vegetables 49
5.12 Spiced Baked Ham 49
5.13 Beef Rolls Stuffed with Spinach and Cheese 50
5.14 Chicken and Avocado Burger 50

6. Side Dishes 51
6.1 Cauliflower Rice 51
6.2 Zucchini Noodles with Garlic 51
6.3 Almond Flour Bread 52
6.4 Cauliflower Mashed Potatoes 52
6.5 Roasted Brussels Sprouts 53
6.6 Grilled Mushrooms 53
6.7 Spinach and Walnut Salad 54
6.8 Grilled Eggplant with Garlic 54
6.9 Radish "Potatoes" 55
6.10 Green Beans with Bacon 55
6.11 Fried Zucchini with Cheese 56
6.12 Flaxseed Crackers 56

6.13 Cabbage Salad with Avocado ... 57
6.14 Baked Sweet Peppers ... 57
7. Sauces and Dressings ... 58
7.1 Mayonnaise ... 58
7.2 Caesar Dressing ... 58
7.3 Pesto ... 59
7.4 Creamy Garlic Sauce ... 59
7.5 Guacamole ... 60
7.6 Garlic Sauce ... 60
7.7 Tartar Sauce ... 61
7.8 Alfredo Sauce ... 61
7.9 Barbecue Sauce ... 62
7.10 Marinara Sauce ... 62
7.11 Hollandaise Sauce ... 63
7.12 Ranch Dressing ... 63
7.13 Salsa ... 64
7.14 Creamy Cheese Sauce ... 64
8. Desserts ... 65
8.1 Chocolate Cake ... 65
8.2 Cheesecake ... 65
8.3 Avocado Ice Cream ... 66
8.4 Almond Flour Cookies ... 66
8.5 Brownies ... 67
8.6 Lemon Cupcakes ... 67
8.7 Apple Pie ... 68
8.8 Coconut Candies ... 68
8.9 Coconut Truffles ... 69
8.10 Marshmallows ... 69
8.11 Cocoa Truffles ... 70
8.12 Nut Cookies ... 70
8.13 Chia Pudding ... 71
8.14 Macarons ... 71
9. Drinks ... 72
9.1 Coffee with Butter ... 72
9.2 Tea with Lemon ... 72
9.3 Coconut Smoothie ... 73
9.4 Avocado Shake ... 73
9.5 Berry Compote ... 73
9.6 Lemonade with Mint ... 74
9.7 Protein Shake ... 74
9.8 Ginger Tea ... 74
9.9 Nut Milkshake ... 75
9.10 Green Smoothie ... 75
9.11 Coconut Milk ... 75
9.12 Almond Milk ... 76
9.13 Hot Chocolate ... 76
9.14 Cinnamon Tea ... 76
Meal Plan for first Week ... 77
Meal Plan for second Week ... 78

Meal Plan for third Week 79
Meal Plan for fourth Week 80
GROCERY LIST for Week 1 81
GROCERY LIST for Week 2 82
GROCERY LIST for Week 3 83
GROCERY LIST for Week 4 84
Reference page 86

Introduction

Welcome to the world of keto cuisine, where healthy eating meets incredible flavor and culinary discoveries! You're about to dive into amazing recipes that will turn your table into a feast for both your eyes and taste buds. This book is your guide to an exciting journey through the ketogenic diet, and I, Kailyn Clark, am thrilled to share my knowledge and passion for cooking with you.

My culinary journey began many years ago, and since then, cooking has become more than just a hobby; it's a true calling. Over the years, I've explored numerous cuisines from around the world, experimented with different ingredients and techniques, all in the pursuit of creating something special and unique. The keto diet was a revelation for me, allowing me to maintain my health while enjoying a wide variety of dishes, all packed with flavor and nutrition.

I know some of you might think that the keto diet is boring or restrictive, but I'm here to debunk those myths. In this book, you'll find over 100 recipes divided into categories: from breakfasts to festive dishes, from snacks to desserts. Each dish has been carefully crafted and personally tested by me, so you can enjoy delicious and healthy food every day. The keto diet is not just a way of eating; it's a lifestyle that opens the door to a new level of energy, health, and enjoyment of food.

Get ready to immerse yourself in a world of culinary discoveries and inspiration! Open the first page, pick a recipe, and start your culinary adventure with me. Whether you're new to the keto diet or a seasoned foodie, I'm confident you'll find something to love in this book. Treat yourself and your loved ones to tasty and healthy dishes that will help you achieve your goals and enjoy every moment at the table.

I, Kailyn Clark, proudly present my cookbook, filled with recipes created with love and a passion for cooking. Let this book be your reliable companion on the path to health and the enjoyment of delicious food. Bon appétit and happy cooking!

Author: Kailyn Clark

Basics of the Keto Diet

The keto diet, also known as the ketogenic diet, is a low-carb, high-fat eating plan. The main goal of the keto diet is to shift your body into a state of ketosis, where it starts using fats as its primary energy source instead of carbohydrates. This is achieved by significantly reducing carbohydrate intake and increasing fat consumption.

Ketosis is a metabolic state where the body breaks down fats for energy instead of carbohydrates. Under normal conditions, the body uses carbohydrates as its main energy source, converting them into glucose. However, when carbohydrate intake is limited, blood glucose levels drop, and the body begins to look for alternative energy sources. At this point, the liver starts processing fats into ketones, which become the new fuel for the body.

Principles of the Keto Diet:

- **Carbohydrate Reduction:** The key principle of the keto diet is to cut carbohydrate intake to 20-50 grams per day. This creates a glucose deficit, leading the body into ketosis.
- **Increased Fat Intake:** To compensate for the energy deficit, fat consumption should be increased to 70-75% of the total diet. Primary sources of fats include avocados, nuts, seeds, oils, meat, and fish.
- **Moderate Protein Consumption:** Proteins should make up about 20-25% of the total diet. Proteins are essential for maintaining muscle mass and performing various functions in the body.

Benefits of the Keto Diet:

- **Weight Loss:** Entering ketosis promotes efficient fat burning, which helps in weight reduction.
- **Blood Sugar Control:** Limiting carbohydrates helps stabilize blood sugar levels, which is particularly beneficial for people with type 2 diabetes.
- **Improved Cognitive Functions:** Ketones are an effective energy source for the brain, which can enhance concentration and memory.
- **Reduced Inflammation:** The keto diet can help reduce inflammation in the body by decreasing the intake of sugar and processed carbohydrates.

Possible Side Effects:

- **Keto Flu:** During the first few weeks of transitioning to the keto diet, many people experience flu-like symptoms such as headaches, fatigue, and nausea. This is due to the body adapting to the new eating regimen.
- **Vitamin and Mineral Deficiency:** Restricting certain foods can lead to deficiencies in some vitamins and minerals. It's recommended to take supplements or include foods rich in essential micronutrients.
- **Constipation:** Due to the low fiber content in some versions of the keto diet, digestive issues can arise. It's important to include fiber-rich vegetables and drink plenty of water.

Foods Allowed on the Keto Diet:

- **Meat and Fish:** Beef, pork, chicken, turkey, salmon, tuna.
- **Dairy Products:** Cheese, butter, cream.
- **Low-Carb Vegetables:** Spinach, broccoli, cauliflower, avocado.
- **Nuts and Seeds:** Almonds, walnuts, chia, flaxseeds.
- **Oils and Fats:** Olive oil, coconut oil, avocado oil.

Foods Prohibited on the Keto Diet:

- **Grains and Grain Products:** Wheat, rice, pasta, bread.
- **Sugars and Sweets:** Sugar, honey, maple syrup, confectionery.
- **Fruits:** Most fruits due to high sugar content, except for berries (in limited amounts).
- **Root Vegetables:** Potatoes, carrots, beets.
- **Low-Fat and Fat-Free Products:** Many low-fat yogurts and cheeses contain added sugars.
- **Alcohol:** Beer, sweet wines, and liqueurs.

The keto diet is a powerful tool for weight loss and overall health improvement. Understanding its basics, how it works, and the potential side effects will help you follow this eating plan effectively. It's important to remember that transitioning to the keto diet requires time and patience, and for best results, consult with a doctor or nutritionist.

Processes in the Body on the Keto Diet

The keto diet significantly impacts metabolic processes in the body. Transitioning from using carbohydrates to fats as the primary energy source involves a series of changes at the cellular and molecular levels. In this chapter, we will explore the key processes occurring in the body during the keto diet and their effects on health and well-being.

Glucose as the Primary Energy Source:

- Under normal conditions, the body uses glucose, derived from carbohydrates, as the main energy source.
- Glucose is quickly absorbed and provides immediate energy for cells.
- Excess glucose is stored as glycogen in the liver and muscles, with any remaining surplus converted into fat.

Transition to Ketosis:

- Reducing carbohydrate intake to 20-50 grams per day lowers blood glucose levels.
- Glycogen stores in the liver and muscles deplete within 2-4 days.
- The body begins using fats as the primary energy source, entering a state of ketosis.

Ketosis Processes:

1. Lipolysis:

- In ketosis, fats from fat stores break down into glycerol and fatty acids.
- Fatty acids are transported to the liver for further processing.

2. Ketogenesis:

- In the liver, fatty acids are converted into ketone bodies: acetoacetate, beta-hydroxybutyrate, and acetone.
- Ketone bodies serve as an alternative energy source for cells, particularly the brain, which cannot use fatty acids directly.

3. Ketone Utilization:

- Ketone bodies travel through the blood to cells, where they are used for energy production in the mitochondria.
- This process is more efficient for extracting energy from fats compared to glucose.

Impact on Hormones and Insulin

- Reduced Insulin Levels:
- Limiting carbohydrates lowers insulin levels in the blood.
- Low insulin levels promote fat burning and prevent fat storage.
- Increased Glucagon Levels:

- Glucagon, a hormone that stimulates fat breakdown, increases with low insulin levels.
- Glucagon also promotes glycogen conversion into glucose and helps maintain blood sugar levels.

Energy Balance and Weight Loss

- Increased Energy Expenditure:
- The keto diet can increase energy expenditure due to the thermogenic effect of proteins and fats.
- Transitioning to ketosis requires more energy for breaking down fats and producing ketones.
- Reduced Appetite:
- Ketones have an appetite-suppressing effect, which can lead to reduced caloric intake.
- Stabilized blood sugar levels prevent drastic hunger spikes.

Impact on the Brain and Cognitive Functions

- Ketones as Brain Energy Source:
- The brain consumes about 20% of the body's energy, and ketones are an efficient energy source for it.
- Using ketones can improve cognitive functions, concentration, and memory.
- Neuroprotective Effect:
- Ketones can protect neurons from oxidative stress and inflammation.
- This can be beneficial for neurodegenerative diseases, such as Alzheimer's.

Impact on the Cardiovascular System

- Reduced Triglyceride Levels:
- The keto diet lowers blood triglyceride levels, improving the lipid profile.
- This reduces the risk of cardiovascular diseases.
- Increased "Good" Cholesterol (HDL) Levels:
- The keto diet increases high-density lipoprotein (HDL) levels, which helps remove "bad" cholesterol (LDL) from the body.

Understanding the metabolic processes and changes occurring in the body during the keto diet helps you better adapt to this eating plan and maximize its benefits. The keto diet not only aids in weight loss but also enhances overall health, cognitive functions, and cardiovascular health. It's essential to consider potential side effects and adaptation processes to achieve the best results.

Tips for Starting and Maintaining Ketosis

Transitioning to a keto diet and maintaining a state of ketosis can be challenging, especially for beginners. In this chapter, we will discuss practical tips and recommendations to help you start the keto diet, stay in ketosis, and reap the maximum benefits from this eating plan.

Starting the Keto Diet

1. Gradual Reduction of Carbohydrates:

- Abruptly cutting carbs can lead to severe keto flu symptoms. Gradually reduce your carbohydrate intake over a few weeks to allow your body time to adjust.

2. Increasing Fat Intake:

- Replace carbs with healthy fats like avocados, nuts, seeds, oils, and fatty meats. Fats should make up about 70-75% of your total diet.

3. Moderate Protein Intake:

- Avoid excessive protein consumption, as excess protein can convert to glucose through gluconeogenesis. Proteins should make up about 20-25% of your total diet.

4. Meal Planning:

- Prepare a weekly menu to avoid accidentally consuming carbs. Plan your meals and snacks around keto-friendly foods.

Maintaining Ketosis

1. Checking Ketone Levels:

- Use urine, blood, or breath test strips to measure ketone levels. This helps you monitor ketosis and make necessary dietary adjustments.

2. Staying Hydrated:

- Maintain a high level of hydration, as the keto diet can lead to water and electrolyte loss. Drink at least 2 liters of water per day.

3. Electrolyte Intake:

- Ensure adequate intake of sodium, potassium, and magnesium. Use supplements or include foods rich in these minerals (e.g., spinach, avocados, nuts).

4. Physical Activity:

- Moderate exercise can speed up the transition to ketosis and improve overall fitness. Regular workouts also help boost ketone levels.

Managing Keto Flu

1. Gradual Adaptation:

- Slowly reduce carbs and increase fats to minimize keto flu symptoms.

2. Hydration and Electrolytes:
- Drink more water and add electrolytes (sodium, potassium, magnesium) to your diet. This helps alleviate headaches, fatigue, and cramps.

3. Nutrient-Dense Foods:
- Include nutrient-rich foods high in vitamins and minerals to maintain overall energy levels and health.

4. Rest and Sleep:
- Ensure adequate rest and sleep to help your body adjust to the new eating plan.

Staying Motivated and Adhering to the Diet

1. Setting Goals:
- Set clear and realistic goals for yourself. These could be weight loss targets, health improvements, or increased energy levels.

2. Keeping a Food Journal:
- Track your intake of carbs, fats, and proteins in a food journal. This helps you stay within the keto diet parameters and monitor your progress.

3. Community Support:
- Join keto communities, online forums, or support groups. Interacting with others on the keto diet can provide valuable advice and support.

4. Variety in Diet:
- Experiment with recipes and add variety to your meals to avoid monotony and keep your interest in the diet.

Starting the keto diet and maintaining ketosis requires time, patience, and discipline. By following these tips, you can successfully adapt to this eating plan, avoid potential side effects, and maximize health benefits. Remember, each body is unique, so listen to your body and consult with a doctor or dietitian if necessary.

Measurement Conversion Tables

Volume Equivalents (Liquid)

US Standard	US Standard (Ounces)	Metric (Approximate)
2 tablespoons	1 fl. oz.	30 ml
¼ cup	2 fl. oz.	60 ml
½ cup	4 fl. oz.	120 ml
1 cup	8 fl. oz.	240 ml
1½ cups	12 fl. oz.	355 ml
2 cups or 1 pint	16 fl. oz.	475 ml
4 cups or 1 quart	32 fl. oz.	1 l
1 gallon	128 fl. oz.	4 L

Oven Temperatures

Fahrenheit (°F)	Celsius (°C) (Approximate)
250°F	120°C
300°F	150°C
325°F	165°C
350°F	180°C
375°F	190°C
400°F	200°C
425°F	220°C
450°F	230°C

Volume Equivalents (Dry)

US Standard	Metric (Approximate)
¼ teaspoon	1 ml
½ teaspoon	2 ml
1 teaspoon	5 ml
1 tablespoon	15 ml
¼ cup	59 ml
⅓ cup	79 ml
½ cup	118 ml
1 cup	235 ml

Weight Equivalents

US Standard	Metric (Approximate)
½ ounce	15 g
1 ounce	30 g
2 ounces	60 g
4 ounces	115 g
8 ounces	225 g
12 ounces	340 g
16 ounces or 1 pound	455 g

1. BREAKFASTS

1.1 Omelet with Avocado and Cheese

Prep time: 5 minutes

Cook time: 10 minutes

Nutritional Value: 350 kcal per serving | 28 g fats | 20 g proteins | 5 g carbs | 3 g fiber | 450 mg sodium

Ingredients (for 2 servings):

- Eggs – 4
- Avocado – 1
- Grated Cheese (Mozzarella or Cheddar) – 3.5 oz
- Butter – 1 tbsp
- Salt – to taste
- Ground Black Pepper – to taste
- Fresh Herbs (parsley, dill) – for garnish

Steps:

1. In a bowl, beat the eggs until smooth, adding a pinch of salt and pepper.
2. Slice the avocado thinly.
3. Heat a skillet over medium heat and melt the butter.
4. Pour the beaten eggs into the skillet and cook, gently stirring, until the omelet starts to set but is still slightly runny on top (about 3-4 minutes).
5. Evenly distribute the avocado slices and grated cheese over the omelet.
6. Fold the omelet in half, covering the filling, and cook for another 1-2 minutes until the cheese is fully melted and the omelet is golden and cooked through.
7. Transfer the omelet to plates, garnish with fresh herbs, and serve immediately.

1.2 Scrambled Eggs with Bacon and Greens

Prep time: 5 minutes

Cook time: 10 minutes

Nutritional Value: 400 kcal per serving | 35 g fats | 20 g proteins | 1 g carbs | 0 g fiber | 800 mg sodium

Ingredients (for 2 servings):

- Eggs – 4
- Bacon – 3.5 oz
- Butter – 1 tbsp
- Fresh Herbs (parsley, dill, green onion) – 1.75 oz
- Salt – to taste
- Ground Black Pepper – to taste

Steps:

1. Cut the bacon into small pieces.
2. Heat a skillet over medium heat and add the bacon. Fry until crispy, about 5 minutes.
3. Transfer the cooked bacon to a paper towel to remove excess fat.
4. In the same skillet, add the butter and melt it.
5. Crack the eggs into the skillet, trying not to break the yolks. Cook over medium heat until the whites are set but the yolks are still runny, about 3-4 minutes.
6. Season with salt and pepper to taste.
7. Place the fried bacon on top of the eggs.
8. Chop the fresh herbs and sprinkle over the dish before serving.

1.3 Almond Flour Pancakes

Prep time: 10 minutes
Cook time: 15 minutes
Nutritional Value: 300 kcal per serving | 28 g fats | 10 g proteins | 5 g carbs | 2 g fiber | 200 mg sodium

Ingredients (for 2 servings):

- Almond Flour – 7 oz
- Eggs – 2
- Heavy Cream (30% fat) – 3.5 fl oz
- Water – 1.7 fl oz
- Butter – 1 tbsp (for frying)
- Baking Powder – 1 tsp
- Salt – a pinch
- Vanilla Extract – 1 tsp (optional)
- Sweetener (Erythritol) – to taste

Steps:

1. In a large bowl, beat the eggs until smooth.
2. Add the cream, water, and vanilla extract (if using). Mix well.
3. In a separate bowl, combine almond flour, baking powder, salt, and sweetener.
4. Gradually add the dry ingredients to the wet mixture, stirring constantly to avoid lumps.
5. Heat a skillet over medium heat and add the butter.
6. Pour a small amount of batter into the skillet, forming pancakes. Fry for 2-3 minutes on each side until golden.
7. Repeat until all the batter is used.

1.4 Coconut Flour Waffles

Prep time: 10 minutes
Cook time: 20 minutes
Nutritional Value: 320 kcal per serving | 27 g fats | 12 g proteins | 6 g carbs | 4 g fiber | 220 mg sodium

Ingredients (for 2 servings):

- Coconut Flour – 1.75 oz
- Eggs – 4
- Heavy Cream (30% fat) – 3.5 fl oz
- Butter – 2 tbsp (melted)
- Baking Powder – 1 tsp
- Vanilla Extract – 1 tsp
- Sweetener (Erythritol) – to taste
- Salt – a pinch

Steps:

1. In a large bowl, beat the eggs until smooth.
2. Add the cream, melted butter, and vanilla extract. Mix well.
3. In a separate bowl, combine coconut flour, baking powder, sweetener, and salt.
4. Gradually add the dry ingredients to the wet mixture, stirring constantly to avoid lumps.
5. Preheat the waffle iron and lightly grease it with butter.
6. Pour the batter into the waffle iron and cook according to the manufacturer's instructions until golden.
7. Repeat until all the batter is used.

1.5 Chia Seed Porridge

Prep time: 10 minutes

Cook time: 2 hours (chilling)

Nutritional Value: 250 kcal per serving | 20 g fats | 5 g proteins | 8 g carbs | 6 g fiber | 100 mg sodium

Ingredients (for 2 servings):

- Chia Seeds – 1.75 oz
- Coconut Milk – 7 fl oz
- Water – 3.5 fl oz
- Vanilla Extract – 1 tsp
- Sweetener (Erythritol) – to taste
- Berries (for garnish) – to taste

Steps:

1. In a bowl, mix chia seeds, coconut milk, water, vanilla extract, and sweetener.
2. Stir well and let sit for 5-10 minutes to allow the seeds to start swelling.
3. Stir again and refrigerate for 2 hours or overnight.
4. Before serving, garnish with berries.

1.6 Scrambled Eggs with Salmon and Spinach

Prep time: 5 minutes

Cook time: 10 minutes

Nutritional Value: 350 kcal per serving | 28 g fats | 20 g proteins | 3 g carbs | 1 g fiber | 450 mg sodium

Ingredients (for 2 servings):

- Eggs – 4
- Smoked Salmon – 3.5 oz
- Fresh Spinach – 3.5 oz
- Butter – 1 tbsp
- Salt – to taste
- Ground Black Pepper – to taste

Steps:

1. Cut the smoked salmon into small pieces.
2. Heat a skillet over medium heat and melt the butter.
3. Add the spinach and cook until wilted, about 2 minutes.
4. In a bowl, beat the eggs and add salt and pepper.
5. Pour the eggs into the skillet and cook, stirring constantly, until the eggs thicken but remain slightly soft.
6. Add the salmon pieces and cook for another minute.
7. Serve immediately.

1.7 Avocado Baked with Egg

Prep time: 5 minutes
Cook time: 15 minutes

Nutritional Value:
300 kcal per serving | 26 g fats | 10 g proteins | 6 g carbs | 4 g fiber | 200 mg sodium

Ingredients (for 2 servings):

- Avocados – 2
- Eggs – 2
- Salt – to taste
- Ground Black Pepper – to taste
- Fresh Herbs (for garnish) – to taste

Steps:

1. Preheat the oven to 400°F (200°C).
2. Cut the avocados in half and remove the pit.
3. Scoop out some of the flesh to create enough space for the egg.
4. Place the avocados on a baking sheet and crack one egg into each avocado half.
5. Season with salt and pepper to taste.
6. Bake in the oven for 12-15 minutes until the egg is set.
7. Garnish with fresh herbs and serve.

1.8 Avocado Cocoa Pudding

Prep time: 10 minutes
Cook time: 1 hour (chilling)

Nutritional Value:
350 kcal per serving | 30 g fats | 5 g proteins | 10 g carbs | 7 g fiber | 150 mg sodium

Ingredients (for 2 servings):

- Avocados – 2
- Cocoa Powder – 2 tbsp
- Coconut Milk – 3.5 fl oz
- Vanilla Extract – 1 tsp
- Sweetener (Erythritol) – to taste

Steps:

1. In a blender, combine avocado flesh, cocoa powder, coconut milk, vanilla extract, and sweetener.
2. Blend until smooth.
3. Divide the pudding into portions and refrigerate for at least 1 hour before serving.

1.7 Avocado Baked with Egg

Prep time: 5 minutes

Cook time: 15 minutes

Nutritional Value: 300 kcal per serving | 26 g fats | 10 g proteins | 6 g carbs | 4 g fiber | 200 mg sodium

Ingredients (for 2 servings):

- Avocados – 2
- Eggs – 2
- Salt – to taste
- Ground Black Pepper – to taste
- Fresh Herbs (for garnish) – to taste

Steps:

1. Preheat the oven to 400°F (200°C).
2. Cut the avocados in half and remove the pit.
3. Scoop out some of the flesh to create enough space for the egg.
4. Place the avocados on a baking sheet and crack one egg into each avocado half.
5. Season with salt and pepper to taste.
6. Bake in the oven for 12-15 minutes until the egg is set.
7. Garnish with fresh herbs and serve.

1.8 Avocado Cocoa Pudding

Prep time: 10 minutes

Cook time: 1 hour (chilling)

Nutritional Value: 350 kcal per serving | 30 g fats | 5 g proteins | 10 g carbs | 7 g fiber | 150 mg sodium

Ingredients (for 2 servings):

- Avocados – 2
- Cocoa Powder – 2 tbsp
- Coconut Milk – 3.5 fl oz
- Vanilla Extract – 1 tsp
- Sweetener (Erythritol) – to taste

Steps:

1. In a blender, combine avocado flesh, cocoa powder, coconut milk, vanilla extract, and sweetener.
2. Blend until smooth.
3. Divide the pudding into portions and refrigerate for at least 1 hour before serving.

1.9 Pancakes with Berries

Prep time: 10 minutes
Cook time: 15 minutes
Nutritional Value: 320 kcal per serving | 28 g fats | 10 g proteins | 6 g carbs | 3 g fiber | 200 mg sodium

Ingredients (for 2 servings):

- Almond Flour – 3.5 oz
- Eggs – 2
- Heavy Cream (30% fat) – 3.5 fl oz
- Water – 1.7 fl oz
- Butter – 1 tbsp (for frying)
- Baking Powder – 1 tsp
- Salt – a pinch
- Vanilla Extract – 1 tsp
- Sweetener (Erythritol) – to taste
- Berries (for serving) – to taste

Steps:

1. In a large bowl, beat the eggs until smooth.
2. Add the cream, water, and vanilla extract. Mix well.
3. In a separate bowl, combine almond flour, baking powder, salt, and sweetener.
4. Gradually add the dry ingredients to the wet mixture, stirring constantly to avoid lumps.
5. Heat a skillet over medium heat and add the butter.
6. Pour a small amount of batter into the skillet, forming pancakes. Fry for 2-3 minutes on each side until golden.
7. Repeat until all the batter is used.
8. Serve the pancakes with berries.

1.10 Frittata with Vegetables and Cheese

Prep time: 10 minutes
Cook time: 15 minutes
Nutritional Value: 350 kcal per serving | 28 g fats | 20 g proteins | 5 g carbs | 2 g fiber | 400 mg sodium

Ingredients (for 2 servings):

- Eggs – 4
- Bell Pepper – 1
- Zucchini – 1
- Cherry Tomatoes – 3.5 oz
- Grated Cheese (Mozzarella or Cheddar) – 3.5 oz
- Butter – 1 tbsp
- Salt – to taste
- Ground Black Pepper – to taste
- Fresh Herbs (parsley, dill) – for garnish

Steps:

1. Cut the bell pepper, zucchini, and cherry tomatoes into small pieces.
2. Heat a skillet over medium heat and melt the butter.
3. Add the chopped vegetables and cook until tender, about 5 minutes.
4. In a bowl, beat the eggs and add salt and pepper.
5. Pour the eggs into the skillet with the vegetables and cook over medium heat until the eggs start to set, about 5 minutes.
6. Sprinkle with grated cheese and cook for another 2-3 minutes until the cheese is melted.
7. Serve the frittata, garnished with fresh herbs.

1.11 Shakshuka with Sausages

Prep time: 10 minutes
Cook time: 20 minutes
Nutritional Value: 400 kcal per serving | 30 g fats | 20 g proteins | 7 g carbs | 2 g fiber | 500 mg sodium

Ingredients (for 2 servings):

- Eggs – 4
- Sausages (e.g., chipolata) – 7 oz
- Tomatoes – 2
- Onion – 1
- Garlic – 2 cloves
- Olive Oil – 2 tbsp
- Paprika – 1 tsp
- Cumin – 1 tsp
- Salt – to taste
- Ground Black Pepper – to taste
- Fresh Herbs (parsley) – for garnish

Steps:

1. Dice the onion and garlic finely. Cut the tomatoes into large chunks.
2. Heat the olive oil in a skillet over medium heat.
3. Add the diced onion and garlic, cook until softened, about 5 minutes.
4. Add the chopped tomatoes, paprika, cumin, salt, and pepper. Cook, stirring, for about 5 minutes until the tomatoes soften.
5. Add the sausages and cook until done, about 10 minutes.
6. Make small wells in the mixture and crack the eggs into the wells.
7. Cover the skillet and cook until the eggs set, about 5 minutes.
8. Garnish with fresh herbs and serve.

1.12 Granola with Coconut and Nuts

Prep time: 10 minutes
Cook time: 20 minutes
Nutritional Value: 450 kcal per serving | 40 g fats | 10 g proteins | 8 g carbs | 5 g fiber | 150 mg sodium

Ingredients (for 2 servings):

- Almonds – 1.75 oz
- Walnuts – 1.75 oz
- Coconut Flakes – 1.75 oz
- Sunflower Seeds – 1 oz
- Flax Seeds – 0.7 oz
- Coconut Oil – 2 tbsp
- Sweetener (Erythritol) – to taste
- Cinnamon – 1 tsp
- Vanilla Extract – 1 tsp

Steps:

1. Preheat the oven to 320°F (160°C).
2. In a bowl, mix almonds, walnuts, coconut flakes, sunflower seeds, and flax seeds.
3. Melt the coconut oil and add it to the nut and seed mixture.
4. Add the sweetener, cinnamon, and vanilla extract, and mix thoroughly.
5. Spread the mixture evenly on a baking sheet lined with parchment paper.
6. Bake in the oven for 15-20 minutes, stirring every 5 minutes, until golden brown.
7. Let the granola cool completely before serving.

1.13 Salad with Eggs and Avocado

Prep time: 10 minutes
Cook time: 10 minutes
Nutritional Value: 350 kcal per serving | 30 g fats | 10 g proteins | 8 g carbs | 5 g fiber | 300 mg sodium

Ingredients (for 2 servings):

- Eggs – 4
- Avocado – 1
- Fresh Cucumber – 1
- Green Onion – 1 oz
- Lettuce Leaves – 3.5 oz
- Olive Oil – 2 tbsp
- Lemon Juice – 1 tbsp
- Salt – to taste
- Ground Black Pepper – to taste

Steps:

1. Hard-boil the eggs, cool, and peel them. Cut the eggs into large pieces.
2. Dice the avocado and cucumber.
3. Finely chop the green onion.
4. Tear the lettuce leaves into pieces.
5. In a large bowl, combine eggs, avocado, cucumber, green onion, and lettuce leaves.
6. Drizzle with olive oil and lemon juice, season with salt and pepper to taste.
7. Toss well and serve.

1.14 Spinach and Avocado Smoothie

Prep time: 5 minutes
Cook time: 5 minutes
Nutritional Value: 250 kcal per serving | 20 g fats | 4 g proteins | 8 g carbs | 6 g fiber | 100 mg sodium

Ingredients (for 2 servings):

- Avocado – 1
- Fresh Spinach – 3.5 oz
- Coconut Milk – 7 fl oz
- Water – 3.5 fl oz
- Lemon Juice – 1 tbsp
- Sweetener (Erythritol) – to taste

Steps:

1. In a blender, combine avocado flesh, fresh spinach, coconut milk, water, lemon juice, and sweetener.
2. Blend until smooth.
3. Pour the smoothie into glasses and serve immediately.

2. SNACKS AND LIGHT MEALS

2.1 Salmon and Avocado Rolls

Prep time: 10 minutes
Cook time: 10 minutes
Nutritional Value: 250 kcal per serving | 18 g fats | 12 g proteins | 5 g carbs | 3 g fiber | 600 mg sodium

Ingredients (for 2 servings):

- Nori Sheets – 2
- Salmon (lightly salted) – 3.5 oz
- Avocado – 1
- Cucumber – 1
- Cream Cheese – 1.75 oz
- Soy Sauce (for serving) – to taste

Steps:

1. Slice the salmon into thin strips.
2. Peel and slice the avocado and cucumber into long strips.
3. Lay the nori sheets on a bamboo mat for rolling.
4. Spread a thin layer of cream cheese on each nori sheet.
5. Place the salmon, avocado, and cucumber strips on the cream cheese.
6. Roll the nori tightly using the bamboo mat.
7. Cut the rolls into pieces and serve with soy sauce.

2.2 Tuna and Egg Salad

Prep time: 10 minutes
Cook time: 10 minutes
Nutritional Value: 300 kcal per serving | 25 g fats | 18 g proteins | 4 g carbs | 2 g fiber | 400 mg sodium

Ingredients (for 2 servings):

- Canned Tuna (in its own juice) – 1 can (5.3 oz)
- Eggs – 2
- Avocado – 1
- Fresh Cucumber – 1
- Lettuce Leaves – 3.5 oz
- Olive Oil – 2 tbsp
- Lemon Juice – 1 tbsp
- Salt – to taste
- Ground Black Pepper – to taste

Steps:

1. Hard-boil the eggs, cool, and peel them. Cut the eggs into large pieces.
2. Dice the avocado and cucumber.
3. Tear the lettuce leaves into pieces.
4. In a large bowl, combine tuna, eggs, avocado, cucumber, and lettuce leaves.
5. Drizzle with olive oil and lemon juice, season with salt and pepper to taste.
6. Toss well and serve.

2.3 Cauliflower Soup

Prep time: 10 minutes

Cook time: 25 minutes

Nutritional Value: 200 kcal per serving | 15 g fats | 4 g proteins | 10 g carbs | 4 g fiber | 300 mg sodium

Ingredients (for 2 servings):

- Cauliflower – 10.5 oz
- Onion – 1
- Garlic – 2 cloves
- Olive Oil – 2 tbsp
- Heavy Cream (30% fat) – 3.5 fl oz
- Vegetable Broth – 17.6 fl oz
- Salt – to taste
- Ground Black Pepper – to taste
- Fresh Herbs (for garnish) – to taste

Steps:

1. Dice the onion and garlic finely.
2. Heat the olive oil in a pot over medium heat.
3. Add the diced onion and garlic, cook until softened, about 5 minutes.
4. Break the cauliflower into florets and add to the pot.
5. Pour in the vegetable broth and bring to a boil.
6. Reduce the heat and simmer until the cauliflower is tender, about 15 minutes.
7. Blend the soup until creamy.
8. Add the cream, salt, and pepper to taste, and mix well.
9. Serve, garnished with fresh herbs.

2.4 Chicken and Avocado Soup

Prep time: 10 minutes

Cook time: 25 minutes

Nutritional Value: 350 kcal per serving | 25 g fats | 20 g proteins | 6 g carbs | 3 g fiber | 400 mg sodium

Ingredients (for 2 servings):

- Chicken Fillet – 7 oz
- Avocado – 1
- Onion – 1
- Garlic – 2 cloves
- Olive Oil – 2 tbsp
- Chicken Broth – 17.6 fl oz
- Heavy Cream (30% fat) – 3.5 fl oz
- Lemon Juice – 1 tbsp
- Salt – to taste
- Ground Black Pepper – to taste
- Fresh Herbs (for garnish) – to taste

Steps:

1. Cut the chicken fillet into small pieces.
2. Dice the onion and garlic finely.
3. Heat the olive oil in a pot over medium heat.
4. Add the diced onion and garlic, cook until softened, about 5 minutes.
5. Add the chicken fillet and cook until golden, about 5 minutes.
6. Pour in the chicken broth and bring to a boil.
7. Reduce the heat and simmer until the chicken is tender, about 15 minutes.
8. Dice the avocado and add to the soup along with the cream and lemon juice.
9. Season with salt and pepper to taste, and mix well.
10. Serve, garnished with fresh herbs.

2.5 Chicken and Cheese Sandwich

Prep time: 10 minutes
Cook time: 10 minutes
Nutritional Value: 400 kcal per serving | 30 g fats | 25 g proteins | 4 g carbs | 2 g fiber | 500 mg sodium

Ingredients (for 2 servings):

- Chicken Fillet – 7 oz
- Cheese (Mozzarella or Cheddar) – 3.5 oz
- Lettuce Leaves – 4
- Avocado – 1
- Keto Mayonnaise – 2 tbsp
- Olive Oil – 1 tbsp
- Salt – to taste
- Ground Black Pepper – to taste

Steps:

1. Cut the chicken fillet into thin slices and season with salt and pepper.
2. Heat the olive oil in a skillet over medium heat and fry the chicken until cooked through, about 5 minutes on each side.
3. Slice the avocado thinly.
4. Place the chicken slices, avocado slices, and grated cheese on each lettuce leaf.
5. Top with mayonnaise and cover with another lettuce leaf.
6. Serve immediately.

2.6 Bacon and Cheese Cupcakes

Prep time: 10 minutes
Cook time: 25 minutes
Nutritional Value: 350 kcal per serving | 30 g fats | 15 g proteins | 2 g carbs | 0 g fiber | 600 mg sodium

Ingredients (for 2 servings):

- Eggs – 4
- Bacon – 3.5 oz
- Grated Cheese (Mozzarella or Cheddar) – 3.5 oz
- Heavy Cream (30% fat) – 1.7 fl oz
- Baking Powder – 1 tsp
- Salt – to taste
- Ground Black Pepper – to taste

Steps:

1. Preheat the oven to 350°F (180°C).
2. Cut the bacon into small pieces and fry until crispy.
3. In a bowl, beat the eggs, add cream, salt, pepper, and baking powder.
4. Add grated cheese and fried bacon, mix well.
5. Pour the mixture into muffin molds, filling them 2/3 full.
6. Bake in the oven for 20-25 minutes until golden brown.
7. Let cool before serving.

2.7 Zucchini Fritters

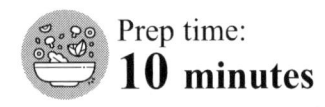

Prep time: **10 minutes**
Cook time: **10 minutes**

Nutritional Value: 250 kcal per serving | 20 g fats | 8 g proteins | 4 g carbs | 2 g fiber | 300 mg sodium

Ingredients (for 2 servings):

- Zucchini – 1
- Egg – 1
- Almond Flour – 1.75 oz
- Grated Cheese (Parmesan) – 1.75 oz
- Salt – to taste
- Ground Black Pepper – to taste
- Olive Oil – 2 tbsp (for frying)

Steps:

1. Grate the zucchini and squeeze out the excess liquid.
2. In a bowl, mix grated zucchini, egg, almond flour, grated cheese, salt, and pepper.
3. Heat olive oil in a skillet over medium heat.
4. Spoon small portions of the batter onto the skillet and fry the fritters for 2-3 minutes on each side until golden brown.
5. Serve hot.

2.8 Caprese Salad with Avocado

Prep time: **10 minutes**
Cook time: **5 minutes**

Nutritional Value: 300 kcal per serving | 25 g fats | 10 g proteins | 6 g carbs | 3 g fiber | 200 mg sodium

Ingredients (for 2 servings):

- Tomatoes – 2
- Mozzarella – 3.5 oz
- Avocado – 1
- Fresh Basil – 0.7 oz
- Olive Oil – 2 tbsp
- Balsamic Vinegar – 1 tbsp
- Salt – to taste
- Ground Black Pepper – to taste

Steps:

1. Slice the tomatoes and mozzarella thinly.
2. Slice the avocado thinly.
3. Arrange the tomatoes, mozzarella, and avocado on a plate, alternating the layers.
4. Sprinkle with fresh basil.
5. Drizzle with olive oil and balsamic vinegar, season with salt and pepper to taste.
6. Serve immediately.

2.9 Cheese Sticks

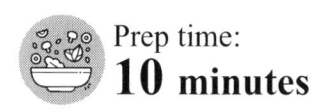

Prep time: 10 minutes
Cook time: 10 minutes
Nutritional Value: 350 kcal per serving | 30 g fats | 15 g proteins | 4 g carbs | 1 g fiber | 400 mg sodium

Ingredients (for 2 servings):

- Grated Cheese (Mozzarella) – 7 oz
- Almond Flour – 1.75 oz
- Egg – 1
- Olive Oil – 2 tbsp (for frying)
- Salt – to taste
- Ground Black Pepper – to taste
- Italian Herbs – to taste

Steps:

1. In a bowl, mix grated cheese, almond flour, egg, salt, pepper, and Italian herbs.
2. Knead the dough and shape it into sticks.
3. Heat olive oil in a skillet over medium heat.
4. Fry the cheese sticks for 2-3 minutes on each side until golden brown.
5. Serve hot.

2.10 Lettuce Leaf Tacos

Prep time: 10 minutes
Cook time: 10 minutes
Nutritional Value: 300 kcal per serving | 25 g fats | 20 g proteins | 5 g carbs | 3 g fiber | 500 mg sodium

Ingredients (for 2 servings):

- Lettuce Leaves – 8
- Ground Meat (beef or chicken) – 7 oz
- Avocado – 1
- Cherry Tomatoes – 3.5 oz
- Grated Cheese (Cheddar) – 1.75 oz
- Sour Cream – 2 tbsp
- Olive Oil – 1 tbsp
- Spices (paprika, cumin, garlic) – to taste
- Salt – to taste
- Ground Black Pepper – to taste

Steps:

1. Heat olive oil in a skillet over medium heat.
2. Add ground meat and spices, cook until done, about 10 minutes.
3. Dice the avocado and cherry tomatoes.
4. Arrange the lettuce leaves on a plate and distribute the meat mixture among them.
5. Top with avocado, tomatoes, grated cheese, and sour cream.
6. Serve immediately.

2.11 Vegetable Omelet Roll

Prep time: 10 minutes
Cook time: 10 minutes
Nutritional Value: 320 kcal per serving | 25 g fat | 15 g protein | 4 g carbs | 2 g fiber | 300 mg sodium

Ingredients (for 2 servings):

- Eggs – 4
- Bell pepper – 1
- Spinach – 1.8 oz
- Butter – 1 tbsp
- Grated cheese (mozzarella or cheddar) – 1 oz
- Salt – to taste
- Ground black pepper – to taste

Steps:

1. Dice the bell pepper into small cubes.
2. Heat the butter in a skillet over medium heat.
3. Add the diced pepper and spinach, cooking until softened, about 5 minutes.
4. In a bowl, beat the eggs, then add salt and pepper.
5. Pour the eggs into the skillet, and cook without stirring until the omelette starts to set, about 5 minutes.
6. Sprinkle the grated cheese on top and cook for another 2-3 minutes, until the cheese melts.
7. Using a spatula, carefully roll the omelette into a roll.
8. Slice the roll into portions and serve.

2.12 Mushroom Cream Soup

Prep time: 10 minutes
Cook time: 25 minutes
Nutritional Value: 350 kcal per serving | 30 g fats | 5 g proteins | 8 g carbs | 2 g fiber | 400 mg sodium

Ingredients (for 2 servings):

- Mushrooms – 7 oz
- Onion – 1
- Garlic – 2 cloves
- Heavy Cream (30% fat) – 7 fl oz
- Vegetable Broth – 17.6 fl oz
- Butter – 2 tbsp
- Salt – to taste
- Ground Black Pepper – to taste
- Fresh Herbs (for garnish) – to taste

Steps:

1. Finely dice the onion and garlic.
2. Slice the mushrooms thinly.
3. Heat the butter in a pot over medium heat.
4. Add the diced onion and garlic, cook until softened, about 5 minutes.
5. Add the sliced mushrooms and cook until they turn golden, about 10 minutes.
6. Pour in the vegetable broth and bring to a boil.
7. Reduce the heat and simmer for 10 minutes.
8. Add the cream, salt, and pepper to taste, and mix well.
9. Serve, garnished with fresh herbs.

2.13 Lettuce Leaf Burgers

Prep time: 10 minutes
Cook time: 10 minutes
Nutritional Value: 400 kcal per serving | 30 g fats | 25 g proteins | 5 g carbs | 3 g fiber | 500 mg sodium

Ingredients (for 2 servings):

- Ground Beef – 7 oz
- Large Lettuce Leaves – 4
- Cheese (Cheddar) – 2 slices
- Avocado – 1
- Tomato – 1
- Red Onion – ½
- Keto Mayonnaise – 2 tbsp
- Olive Oil – 1 tbsp
- Salt – to taste
- Ground Black Pepper – to taste

Steps:

1. Season the ground beef with salt and pepper, and shape it into two patties.
2. Heat olive oil in a skillet over medium heat and fry the patties until cooked through, about 5 minutes on each side.
3. In the last minutes of frying, place the cheese slices on the patties to melt.
4. Slice the avocado and tomato thinly, and cut the onion into rings.
5. Place two large lettuce leaves on each plate.
6. Top the lettuce with a patty with melted cheese, then add slices of avocado, tomato, and onion.
7. Add mayonnaise to taste and cover with another lettuce leaf.
8. Serve immediately.

2.14 Tomato and Basil Bruschetta

Prep time: 10 minutes
Cook time: 20 minutes
Nutritional Value: 350 kcal per serving | 28 g fats | 10 g proteins | 7 g carbs | 3 g fiber | 300 mg sodium

Ingredients (for 2 servings):

- Almond Flour – 3.5 oz
- Eggs – 2
- Cheese (Parmesan) – 1.75 oz
- Tomatoes – 2
- Fresh Basil – 0.7 oz
- Olive Oil – 2 tbsp
- Garlic – 1 clove
- Salt – to taste
- Ground Black Pepper – to taste

Steps:

1. In a bowl, mix almond flour, eggs, and grated Parmesan to make a dough.
2. Preheat the oven to 350°F (180°C) and place the dough on a baking sheet, forming flatbread.
3. Bake in the oven for 15-20 minutes until golden brown.
4. Dice the tomatoes, and finely chop the basil and garlic.
5. In a bowl, mix the diced tomatoes, basil, garlic, olive oil, salt, and pepper.
6. Place the mixture on the baked flatbread before serving.
7. Serve immediately.

3. MAIN DISHES

3.1 Baked Beef with Rosemary

Prep time: 10 minutes
Cook time: 40 minutes

Nutritional Value:
450 kcal per serving | 35 g fats | 30 g proteins | 1 g carbs | 0 g fiber | 600 mg sodium

Ingredients (for 2 servings):

- Beef Fillet – 14 oz
- Fresh Rosemary – 2 sprigs
- Garlic – 3 cloves
- Olive Oil – 2 tbsp
- Salt – to taste
- Ground Black Pepper – to taste

Steps:

1. Preheat the oven to 400°F (200°C).
2. In a small bowl, mix olive oil, finely chopped garlic, salt, and pepper.
3. Rub the beef with the oil and spice mixture.
4. Place the rosemary sprigs on the beef and wrap it in foil.
5. Bake in the oven for 25-30 minutes, then remove the foil and bake for another 10 minutes to form a crust.
6. Let the meat rest for 5 minutes before slicing.
7. Serve sliced.

3.2 Almond Crust Pizza

Prep time: 10 minutes
Cook time: 25 minutes

Nutritional Value:
400 kcal per serving | 35 g fats | 20 g proteins | 7 g carbs | 3 g fiber | 450 mg sodium

Ingredients (for 2 servings):

For the crust:
- Almond Flour – 5.3 oz
- Egg – 1
- Grated Cheese (Mozzarella) – 3.5 oz
- Baking Powder – 1 tsp
- Salt – to taste

For the topping:
- Tomatoes – 2
- Mozzarella – 3.5 oz
- Fresh Basil – 0.7 oz
- Olive Oil – 1 tbsp
- Salt – to taste
- Ground Black Pepper – to taste

Steps:

1. Preheat the oven to 350°F (180°C).
2. In a bowl, mix almond flour, egg, grated cheese, baking powder, and salt until a dough forms.
3. Place the dough on a baking sheet, shaping it into a round or rectangular crust.
4. Bake the crust for 10-15 minutes until golden.
5. Slice the tomatoes and mozzarella.
6. Place the sliced tomatoes, mozzarella, and fresh basil on the crust.
7. Drizzle with olive oil, salt, and pepper.
8. Bake for another 10 minutes until the cheese melts.
9. Serve hot.

3.3 Chicken Breasts in Creamy Sauce

Prep time: 10 minutes

Cook time: 20 minutes

Nutritional Value: 450 kcal per serving | 35 g fats | 30 g proteins | 4 g carbs | 0 g fiber | 600 mg sodium

Ingredients (for 2 servings):

- Chicken Breasts – 2
- Heavy Cream (30% fat) – 7 fl oz
- Garlic – 2 cloves
- Grated Cheese (Parmesan) – 1.75 oz
- Butter – 1 tbsp
- Salt – to taste
- Ground Black Pepper – to taste
- Fresh Parsley (for garnish) – to taste

Steps:

1. Season the chicken breasts with salt and pepper.
2. Heat the butter in a skillet over medium heat.
3. Fry the chicken breasts until golden brown, about 5 minutes on each side.
4. Reduce the heat, add finely chopped garlic, and cook for another minute.
5. Pour in the cream and add the grated Parmesan, stirring well.
6. Simmer the chicken breasts in the creamy sauce over low heat until the sauce thickens, about 10 minutes.
7. Serve, garnished with fresh parsley.

3.4 Pork in Barbecue Sauce

Prep time: 15 minutes

Cook time: 40 minutes

Nutritional Value: 500 kcal per serving | 40 g fats | 25 g proteins | 6 g carbs | 2 g fiber | 700 mg sodium

Ingredients (for 2 servings):

- Pork (shoulder or neck) – 14 oz
- Barbecue Sauce – 3.5 fl oz
- Olive Oil – 2 tbsp
- Salt – to taste
- Ground Black Pepper – to taste

For the sauce:

- Tomato Paste – 1.75 oz
- Apple Cider Vinegar – 2 tbsp
- Worcestershire Sauce – 1 tbsp
- Erythritol – 1 tbsp
- Smoked Paprika – 1 tsp
- Garlic Powder – 1 tsp
- Onion Powder – 1 tsp
- Salt – to taste

Steps:

1. Prepare the barbecue sauce by mixing all the sauce ingredients in a small saucepan and bringing to a boil. Reduce the heat and simmer for 10 minutes, stirring.
2. Season the pork with salt and pepper.
3. Heat olive oil in a skillet over medium heat.
4. Fry the pork until golden brown, about 5 minutes on each side.
5. Brush the pork with barbecue sauce and transfer to an oven preheated to 350°F (180°C).
6. Bake for 25-30 minutes until cooked through.
7. Slice the pork and serve with the remaining sauce.

3.5 Grilled Salmon with Lemon and Dill

Prep time: 5 minutes

Cook time: 12 minutes

Nutritional Value:
350 kcal per serving | 25 g fats | 30 g proteins | 2 g carbs | 0 g fiber | 200 mg sodium

Ingredients (for 2 servings):

- Salmon Fillet – 14 oz
- Lemon – 1
- Fresh Dill – 0.7 oz
- Olive Oil – 2 tbsp
- Salt – to taste
- Ground Black Pepper – to taste

Steps:

1. Preheat the grill to medium temperature.
2. Rub the salmon fillet with olive oil, salt, and pepper.
3. Slice the lemon into thin rounds.
4. Place the salmon fillet on the grill, skin-side down, and top with lemon slices.
5. Grill the salmon for about 10-12 minutes until it is opaque and easily flakes with a fork.
6. Chop the fresh dill and sprinkle it over the cooked fillet before serving.
7. Serve with lemon slices.

3.6 Spaghetti with Meat Sauce

Prep time: 10 minutes

Cook time: 25 minutes

Nutritional Value:
400 kcal per serving | 30 g fats | 25 g proteins | 10 g carbs | 3 g fiber | 450 mg sodium

Ingredients (for 2 servings):

For the spaghetti:
- Zucchini – 2
- Olive Oil – 1 tbsp

For the meat sauce:
- Ground Beef – 7 oz
- Onion – 1
- Garlic – 2 cloves
- Tomato Paste – 3.5 oz
- Olive Oil – 1 tbsp
- Salt – to taste
- Ground Black Pepper – to taste
- Italian Herbs – to taste

Steps:

1. Slice the zucchini into thin strips using a vegetable peeler.
2. Heat olive oil in a skillet over medium heat and fry the zucchini strips for 2-3 minutes until soft. Set aside.
3. Finely dice the onion and garlic.
4. In another skillet, heat olive oil and fry the onion and garlic until soft, about 5 minutes.
5. Add the ground beef and cook, stirring, until fully cooked, about 10 minutes.
6. Add the tomato paste, salt, pepper, and Italian herbs. Simmer on low heat for another 10 minutes.
7. Serve the zucchini spaghetti with the meat sauce.

3.7 Baked Cod with Broccoli

Prep time: 10 minutes
Cook time: 25 minutes

Nutritional Value:
300 kcal per serving | 15 g fats | 30 g proteins | 5 g carbs | 3 g fiber | 400 mg sodium

Ingredients (for 2 servings):

- Cod Fillet – 14 oz
- Broccoli – 10.5 oz
- Olive Oil – 2 tbsp
- Garlic – 2 cloves
- Lemon Juice – 1 tbsp
- Salt – to taste
- Ground Black Pepper – to taste
- Fresh Herbs (for garnish) – to taste

Steps:

1. Preheat the oven to 400°F (200°C).
2. Cut the broccoli into florets and finely chop the garlic.
3. Place the cod and broccoli on a baking sheet, drizzle with olive oil and lemon juice.
4. Sprinkle with chopped garlic, salt, and pepper.
5. Bake in the oven for 20-25 minutes until the fish is cooked through and the broccoli is tender.
6. Garnish with fresh herbs before serving.

3.8 Zucchini Lasagna

Prep time: 15 minutes
Cook time: 30 minutes

Nutritional Value:
400 kcal per serving | 25 g fats | 30 g proteins | 10 g carbs | 3 g fiber | 450 mg sodium

Ingredients (for 2 servings):

- Zucchini – 2
- Ground Beef – 7 oz
- Onion – 1
- Garlic – 2 cloves
- Tomato Paste – 3.5 oz
- Ricotta – 3.5 oz
- Grated Cheese (Mozzarella) – 3.5 oz
- Olive Oil – 1 tbsp
- Salt – to taste
- Ground Black Pepper – to taste
- Italian Herbs – to taste

Steps:

1. Preheat the oven to 350°F (180°C).
2. Slice the zucchini into thin sheets using a vegetable peeler.
3. Finely dice the onion and garlic.
4. Heat olive oil in a skillet and fry the onion and garlic until soft, about 5 minutes.
5. Add the ground beef and cook until done, about 10 minutes.
6. Add the tomato paste, salt, pepper, and Italian herbs, simmer for another 5 minutes.
7. In a baking dish, layer zucchini slices, then meat sauce, then ricotta. Repeat layers, ending with grated mozzarella.
8. Bake in the oven for 25-30 minutes until golden brown.
9. Serve hot.

3.9 Beef Fajitas

Prep time: 15 minutes
Cook time: 15 minutes
Nutritional Value: 400 kcal per serving | 30 g fats | 25 g proteins | 10 g carbs | 4 g fiber | 500 mg sodium

Ingredients (for 2 servings):

- Beef Steak (Fillet) – 10.5 oz
- Bell Pepper – 1
- Onion – 1
- Avocado – 1
- Lettuce Leaves – 4
- Olive Oil – 2 tbsp
- Lime Juice – 1 tbsp
- Paprika – 1 tsp
- Cumin – 1 tsp
- Salt – to taste
- Ground Black Pepper – to taste

Steps:

1. Slice the beef steak into thin strips.
2. In a large bowl, mix olive oil, lime juice, paprika, cumin, salt, and pepper. Marinate the beef in this mixture for 15 minutes.
3. Slice the bell pepper and onion into thin strips.
4. Heat a skillet over medium heat and fry the beef until done, about 5-7 minutes.
5. Add the sliced pepper and onion, cook for another 5 minutes until the vegetables are soft.
6. Slice the avocado.
7. Serve the fajitas on lettuce leaves with avocado slices.

3.10 Pork and Cabbage Stew

Prep time: 10 minutes
Cook time: 40 minutes
Nutritional Value: 450 kcal per serving | 30 g fats | 25 g proteins | 12 g carbs | 5 g fiber | 600 mg sodium

Ingredients (for 2 servings):

- Pork (Shoulder) – 10.5 oz
- White Cabbage – 10.5 oz
- Onion – 1
- Carrot – 1
- Garlic – 2 cloves
- Olive Oil – 2 tbsp
- Tomato Paste – 2 tbsp
- Water – 7 fl oz
- Salt – to taste
- Ground Black Pepper – to taste
- Bay Leaf – 1

Steps:

1. Cut the pork into cubes.
2. Finely dice the onion, carrot, and garlic.
3. Chop the cabbage into large pieces.
4. In a large pot, heat the olive oil and fry the pork until golden, about 5 minutes.
5. Add the onion, carrot, and garlic, cook until soft, about 5 minutes.
6. Add the tomato paste and water, stir well.
7. Add the cabbage, bay leaf, salt, and pepper. Simmer on low heat for about 30 minutes until the pork and cabbage are tender.
8. Serve hot.

3.11 Chicken Curry

Prep time: 10 minutes
Cook time: 25 minutes
Nutritional Value: 400 kcal per serving | 30 g fats | 25 g proteins | 5 g carbs | 2 g fiber | 450 mg sodium

Ingredients (for 2 servings):

- Chicken Fillet – 10.5 oz
- Coconut Milk – 7 fl oz
- Onion – 1
- Garlic – 2 cloves
- Fresh Ginger – 1-inch piece
- Curry Powder – 1 tbsp
- Coconut Oil – 2 tbsp
- Salt – to taste
- Ground Black Pepper – to taste
- Fresh Cilantro (for garnish) – to tasteSalt – to taste
- Ground Black Pepper – to taste

Steps:

1. Cut the chicken fillet into cubes.
2. Finely dice the onion and garlic, and grate the ginger.
3. Heat the coconut oil in a large skillet over medium heat.
4. Add the onion, garlic, and ginger, and cook until soft, about 5 minutes.
5. Add the chicken fillet and curry powder, and cook until the chicken is done, about 10 minutes.
6. Pour in the coconut milk, add salt and pepper, and simmer on low heat for another 10 minutes.
7. Serve garnished with fresh cilantro.

3.12 Beef Stew with Mushrooms

Prep time: 10 minutes
Cook time: 35 minutes
Nutritional Value: 450 kcal per serving | 35 g fats | 25 g proteins | 6 g carbs | 2 g fiber | 500 mg sodium

Ingredients (for 2 servings):

- Beef Steak (Fillet) – 10.5 oz
- Mushrooms – 7 oz
- Onion – 1
- Garlic – 2 cloves
- Butter – 2 tbsp
- Heavy Cream (30% fat) – 3.5 fl oz
- Water – 3.5 fl oz
- Salt – to taste
- Ground Black Pepper – to taste
- Fresh Parsley (for garnish) – to taste

Steps:

1. Cut the beef into cubes.
2. Finely dice the onion, garlic, and mushrooms.
3. Heat the butter in a large pot over medium heat.
4. Add the onion and garlic, and cook until soft, about 5 minutes.
5. Add the beef and cook until golden brown, about 10 minutes.
6. Add the mushrooms and cook for another 5 minutes.
7. Pour in the cream and water, add salt and pepper, and simmer on low heat for about 20 minutes until the beef is tender.
8. Serve garnished with fresh parsley.

3.13 Chicken Fricassee with Vegetables

Prep time: 10 minutes
Cook time: 30 minutes

Nutritional Value:
400 kcal per serving | 30 g fats | 25 g proteins | 8 g carbs | 3 g fiber | 400 mg sodium

Ingredients (for 2 servings):

- Chicken Fillet – 10.5 oz
- Cauliflower – 7 oz
- Broccoli – 7 oz
- Carrot – 1
- Heavy Cream (30% fat) – 7 fl oz
- Butter – 2 tbsp
- Garlic – 2 cloves
- Onion – 1
- Salt – to taste
- Ground Black Pepper – to taste
- Fresh Herbs (for garnish) – to taste

Steps:

1. Cut the chicken fillet into cubes.
2. Finely dice the onion and garlic.
3. Cut the cauliflower and broccoli into florets, and slice the carrot into thin rounds.
4. Heat the butter in a large skillet over medium heat.
5. Add the onion and garlic, and cook until soft, about 5 minutes.
6. Add the chicken fillet and cook until golden brown, about 10 minutes.
7. Add the carrot, cauliflower, and broccoli, and cook for another 5 minutes.
8. Pour in the cream, add salt and pepper, and simmer on low heat for another 10 minutes.
9. Serve garnished with fresh herbs.

3.14 Turkey Kebab

Prep time: 10 minutes
Cook time: 20 minutes

Nutritional Value:
350 kcal per serving | 25 g fats | 30 g proteins | 2 g carbs | 0 g fiber | 500 mg sodium

Ingredients (for 2 servings):

- Turkey Fillet – 14 oz
- Olive Oil – 2 tbsp
- Lemon Juice – 1 tbsp
- Garlic – 2 cloves
- Paprika – 1 tsp
- Cumin – 1 tsp
- Salt – to taste
- Ground Black Pepper – to taste
- Fresh Herbs (for serving) – to taste

Steps:

1. Cut the turkey fillet into cubes.
2. In a large bowl, mix olive oil, lemon juice, minced garlic, paprika, cumin, salt, and pepper.
3. Marinate the turkey in this mixture for 20 minutes.
4. Preheat the grill to medium temperature.
5. Skewer the turkey pieces onto skewers.
6. Grill the kebabs, turning every 5 minutes, until fully cooked, about 15-20 minutes.
7. Serve with fresh herbs.

4. FISH AND SEAFOOD

4.1 Salmon Fillet with Lemon Butter and Asparagus

Prep time: 10 minutes
Cook time: 20 minutes
Nutritional Value: 400 kcal per serving | 28 g fats | 35 g proteins | 5 g carbs | 3 g fiber | 250 mg sodium

Ingredients (for 2 servings):

- Salmon Fillet – 10.5 oz
- Asparagus – 7 oz
- Lemon – 1
- Butter – 1.8 oz
- Olive Oil – 1 tbsp
- Garlic – 2 cloves
- Salt – to taste
- Ground Black Pepper – to taste

Steps:

1. Preheat the oven to 350°F (180°C).
2. Arrange the asparagus on a baking sheet, drizzle with olive oil, and season with salt and pepper.
3. Place the salmon fillet on top of the asparagus.
4. Crush and finely chop the garlic.
5. In a small saucepan, melt the butter, add the garlic and juice from half a lemon. Bring to a boil and cook for 1-2 minutes.
6. Pour the lemon-garlic butter over the salmon.
7. Bake in the oven for 15-20 minutes until the salmon is cooked through.
8. Serve hot, garnished with lemon slices.

4.2 Shrimp in Garlic Sauce

Prep time: 10 minutes
Cook time: 5 minutes
Nutritional Value: 250 kcal per serving | 18 g fats | 20 g proteins | 2 g carbs | 0 g fiber | 400 mg sodium

Ingredients (for 2 servings):

- Shrimp (peeled) – 10.5 oz
- Garlic – 4 cloves
- Butter – 1.8 oz
- Olive Oil – 1 tbsp
- Lemon Juice – 2 tbsp
- Fresh Parsley (chopped) – 2 tbsp
- Salt – to taste
- Ground Black Pepper – to taste

Steps:

1. Crush and finely chop the garlic.
2. In a skillet over medium heat, heat the olive oil and butter.
3. Add the garlic and sauté until fragrant, about 1 minute.
4. Add the shrimp and cook, stirring, for about 3-4 minutes until they turn pink and opaque.
5. Add the lemon juice, salt, and pepper, and stir well.
6. Remove from heat and sprinkle with chopped parsley.
7. Serve hot.

4.3 Baked Cod with Broccoli and Cheese

Prep time: 10 minutes

Cook time: 25 minutes

Nutritional Value: 350 kcal per serving | 25 g fats | 30 g proteins | 5 g carbs | 2 g fiber | 300 mg sodium

Ingredients (for 2 servings):

- Cod Fillet – 10.5 oz
- Broccoli – 7 oz
- Cheddar Cheese – 3.5 oz
- Butter – 1 oz
- Heavy Cream (30% fat) – 3.5 fl oz
- Salt – to taste
- Ground Black Pepper – to taste

Steps:

1. Preheat the oven to 350°F (180°C).
2. Separate the broccoli into florets and sauté in butter for 3-4 minutes.
3. Place the broccoli in a baking dish.
4. Place the cod fillet on top of the broccoli, season with salt and pepper.
5. Pour the cream over and sprinkle with grated cheese.
6. Bake in the oven for 20-25 minutes until the fish is cooked through and the cheese is melted.
7. Serve hot.

4.4 Sea Bass with Olives and Tomatoes

Prep time: 10 minutes

Cook time: 25 minutes

Nutritional Value: 300 kcal per serving | 20 g fats | 25 g proteins | 6 g carbs | 2 g fiber | 250 mg sodium

Ingredients (for 2 servings):

- Sea Bass Fillet – 10.5 oz
- Cherry Tomatoes – 7 oz
- Olives (pitted) – 1.8 oz
- Garlic – 2 cloves
- Olive Oil – 2 tbsp
- Salt – to taste
- Ground Black Pepper – to taste
- Fresh Basil – for garnish

Steps:

1. Preheat the oven to 350°F (180°C).
2. Halve the cherry tomatoes and finely chop the garlic.
3. Place the sea bass fillet in a baking dish, season with salt and pepper.
4. Arrange the cherry tomatoes and olives around the fish.
5. Drizzle with olive oil and sprinkle with garlic.
6. Bake in the oven for 20-25 minutes until the fish is cooked through.
7. Garnish with fresh basil before serving.

4.5 Grilled Tuna with Avocado

Prep time: 10 minutes
Cook time: 6 minutes
Nutritional Value: 350 kcal per serving | 25 g fats | 30 g proteins | 5 g carbs | 3 g fiber | 200 mg sodium

Ingredients (for 2 servings):

- Tuna Fillet – 10.5 oz
- Avocado – 1
- Lemon – 1
- Olive Oil – 2 tbsp
- Garlic – 1 clove
- Salt – to taste
- Ground Black Pepper – to taste

Steps:

1. Preheat the grill to medium temperature.
2. Rub the tuna fillet with olive oil, salt, and pepper.
3. Grill the tuna for 2-3 minutes on each side to the desired doneness.
4. Slice the avocado and lemon thinly.
5. Place the tuna on a plate, top with avocado slices, and drizzle with lemon juice.
6. Garnish with finely grated garlic.
7. Serve hot.

4.6 Squid and Cucumber Salad

Prep time: 10 minutes
Cook time: 5 minutes
Nutritional Value: 150 kcal per serving | 10 g fats | 10 g proteins | 4 g carbs | 2 g fiber | 150 mg sodium

Ingredients (for 2 servings):

- Squid (cleaned) – 7 oz
- Cucumber – 1
- Red Onion – 1/2
- Lemon Juice – 1 tbsp
- Olive Oil – 2 tbsp
- Salt – to taste
- Ground Black Pepper – to taste
- Fresh Herbs – for garnish

Steps:

1. Boil water in a pot and cook the squid for 2-3 minutes, then cool and cut into rings.
2. Cut the cucumber into thin strips.
3. Slice the red onion into thin half-rings.
4. In a bowl, combine the squid, cucumber, and onion.
5. Drizzle with lemon juice and olive oil, season with salt and pepper to taste.
6. Mix well and garnish with fresh herbs before serving.

The Ultimate Keto Diet After 60

4.7 Steamed Salmon with Green Beans

Prep time: **5 minutes**
Cook time: **12 minutes**

Nutritional Value:
250 kcal per serving | 15 g fats | 25 g proteins | 6 g carbs | 3 g fiber | 200 mg sodium

Ingredients (for 2 servings):

- Salmon Fillet – 10.5 oz
- Green Beans – 7 oz
- Lemon – 1
- Salt – to taste
- Ground Black Pepper – to taste
- Fresh Dill – for garnish

Steps:

1. Prepare a steamer.
2. Cut the salmon fillet into portions, season with salt and pepper.
3. Place the salmon in the steamer and cook for 10-12 minutes until done.
4. Steam the green beans simultaneously for about 5-7 minutes.
5. Arrange the salmon and green beans on a plate.
6. Drizzle with lemon juice and garnish with fresh dill before serving.

4.8 Fish Soup with Salmon

Prep time: **10 minutes**
Cook time: **25 minutes**

Nutritional Value:
200 kcal per serving | 8 g fats | 25 g proteins | 8 g carbs | 2 g fiber | 300 mg sodium

Ingredients (for 2 servings):

- Salmon (or trout) – 10.5 oz
- Carrot – 1
- Onion – 1
- Potato – 1 (optional)
- Bay Leaf – 2
- Water – 4 cups
- Salt – to taste
- Ground Black Pepper – to taste
- Fresh Herbs (dill or parsley) – for garnish

Steps:

1. Cut the salmon into portions.
2. Dice the carrot and potato, finely chop the onion.
3. In a pot, bring water to a boil, add the carrot, potato, and onion, and cook for 10-15 minutes until the vegetables are tender.
4. Add the fish and bay leaf, season with salt and pepper.
5. Cook for another 10 minutes until the fish is done.
6. Remove the bay leaf and serve the soup garnished with fresh herbs.

4.9 Shrimp Cocktail with Avocado

Prep time: 10 minutes
Cook time: 3 minutes

Nutritional Value:
250 kcal per serving | 18 g fats | 20 g proteins | 6 g carbs | 4 g fiber | 200 mg sodium

Ingredients (for 2 servings):

- Shrimp (peeled) – 7 oz
- Avocado – 1
- Lemon Juice – 1 tbsp
- Olive Oil – 1 tbsp
- Salt – to taste
- Ground Black Pepper – to taste
- Fresh Herbs (dill or parsley) – for garnish

Steps:

1. Boil the shrimp in salted water for 2-3 minutes until done, then cool.
2. Dice the avocado and drizzle with lemon juice to prevent browning.
3. In a bowl, combine the shrimp and avocado.
4. Drizzle with olive oil, season with salt and pepper to taste.
5. Mix well and garnish with fresh herbs before serving.

4.10 Baked Trout with Lemon and Herbs

Prep time: 10 minutes
Cook time: 25 minutes

Nutritional Value:
300 kcal per serving | 20 g fats | 25 g proteins | 3 g carbs | 1 g fiber | 150 mg sodium

Ingredients (for 2 servings):

- Trout – 1 (about 1 lb)
- Lemon – 1
- Garlic – 3 cloves
- Olive Oil – 2 tbsp
- Fresh Rosemary – 2 sprigs
- Salt – to taste
- Ground Black Pepper – to taste

Steps:

1. Preheat the oven to 350°F (180°C).
2. Clean the trout, season with salt and pepper inside and out.
3. Slice the lemon thinly.
4. Crush and finely chop the garlic.
5. Place lemon slices and rosemary sprigs inside the fish.
6. Place the trout on a baking sheet lined with parchment paper, drizzle with olive oil, and sprinkle with garlic.
7. Bake in the oven for 20-25 minutes until done.
8. Serve hot, garnished with additional lemon slices and fresh herbs.

4.11 Fish and Avocado Rolls

Prep time: 15 minutes
Cook time: 5 minutes

Nutritional Value:
200 kcal per serving | 15 g fats | 10 g proteins | 6 g carbs | 3 g fiber | 250 mg sodium

Ingredients (for 2 servings):

- Nori Sheets – 2
- Fish (salmon or tuna, raw) – 3.5 oz
- Avocado – 1
- Cucumber – 1
- Cauliflower (for "rice" mixture) – 7 oz
- Cream Cheese – 2 oz
- Soy Sauce (sugar-free) – to taste
- Wasabi – to taste

Steps:

1. Process the cauliflower in a blender until it resembles rice.
2. Lightly sauté the cauliflower in a dry pan until soft, then let it cool.
3. Cut the fish, avocado, and cucumber into thin strips.
4. Lay a nori sheet on a bamboo sushi mat.
5. Spread an even layer of cauliflower rice over the nori sheet, leaving the top edge free (about 1 cm).
6. Place strips of fish, avocado, and cucumber on the bottom edge of the nori sheet, and add a bit of cream cheese.
7. Roll up the nori sheet with the filling using the sushi mat.
8. Cut the sushi roll into portions.
9. Serve with soy sauce and wasabi.

4.12 Crab Cakes with Tartar Sauce

Prep time: 10 minutes
Cook time: 10 minutes

Nutritional Value:
300 kcal per serving | 20 g fats | 20 g proteins | 5 g carbs | 2 g fiber | 400 mg sodium

Ingredients (for 2 servings):

- Crab Meat – 7 oz
- Egg – 1
- Almond Flour – 2 tbsp
- Green Onion (finely chopped) – 1 tbsp
- Mayonnaise (keto) – 2 tbsp
- Dijon Mustard – 1 tsp
- Lemon Juice – 1 tbsp
- Salt – to taste
- Ground Black Pepper – to taste
- Olive Oil – for frying

For Tartar Sauce:

- Mayonnaise (keto) – 4 tbsp
- Pickles (finely chopped) – 1 tbsp
- Capers (finely chopped) – 1 tsp
- Lemon Juice – 1 tbsp
- Salt – to taste
- Ground Black Pepper – to taste

Steps:

1. In a bowl, mix the crab meat, egg, almond flour, green onion, mayonnaise, mustard, lemon juice, salt, and pepper until well combined.
2. Form the mixture into cakes.
3. Heat olive oil in a pan over medium heat and fry the cakes for 3-4 minutes on each side until golden brown.
4. For the tartar sauce, mix all the ingredients in a small bowl.
5. Serve the crab cakes with tartar sauce.

4.13 Mussels in Cream Sauce

Prep time: 10 minutes

Cook time: 10 minutes

Nutritional Value:
350 kcal per serving | 28 g fats | 18 g proteins | 6 g carbs | 1 g fiber | 500 mg sodium

Ingredients (for 2 servings):

- Mussels – 1 lb
- Butter – 2 oz
- Garlic – 3 cloves
- Cream (30% fat) – 7 oz
- White Wine (optional) – 2 oz
- Parsley (fresh, chopped) – 2 tbsp
- Salt – to taste
- Ground Black Pepper – to taste

Steps:

1. Melt the butter in a large pan over medium heat.
2. Crush and finely chop the garlic, add to the pan, and sauté until fragrant, about 1 minute.
3. Add the mussels and white wine (if using), cook for 2-3 minutes until the mussels begin to open.
4. Add the cream, salt, and pepper, and cook for another 5-7 minutes until the sauce thickens.
5. Sprinkle with chopped parsley before serving.
6. Serve hot.6. Place strips of fish, avocado, and cucumber on the bottom edge of the nori sheet, and add a bit of cream cheese.
7. Roll up the nori sheet with the filling using the sushi mat.
8. Cut the sushi roll into portions.
9. Serve with soy sauce and wasabi.

4.14 Fish and Avocado Ceviche

Prep time: 10 minutes

Cook time: 20 minutes

Nutritional Value:
250 kcal per serving | 18 g fats | 15 g proteins | 8 g carbs | 4 g fiber | 200 mg sodium

Ingredients (for 2 servings):

- White Fish (sea bass or cod) – 7 oz
- Avocado – 1
- Lemon Juice – 2 tbsp
- Lime Juice – 2 tbsp
- Red Onion – 1/4
- Tomato – 1
- Cilantro (fresh, chopped) – 2 tbsp
- Salt – to taste
- Ground Black Pepper – to taste

Steps:

1. Cut the fish into small cubes and place in a bowl.
2. Add the lemon and lime juices to cover the fish completely. Marinate in the refrigerator for 15-20 minutes until the fish turns white and opaque.
3. Dice the avocado, red onion, and tomato.
4. Add the avocado, onion, tomato, and cilantro to the fish and mix well.
5. Season with salt and pepper to taste.
6. Serve the ceviche chilled.

5. MEAT AND POULTRY

5.1 Chicken Breasts with Broccoli and Cheese

Prep time: 10 minutes
Cook time: 20 minutes
Nutritional Value: 350 kcal per serving | 25 g fats | 30 g proteins | 6 g carbs | 3 g fiber | 250 mg sodium

Ingredients (for 2 servings):

- Chicken Breasts – 10 oz (300 g)
- Broccoli – 7 oz (200 g)
- Cheese (Cheddar or Mozzarella) – 3.5 oz (100 g)
- Butter – 1 oz (30 g)
- Cream (30% fat) – 3.5 oz (100 ml)
- Garlic – 2 cloves
- Salt – to taste
- Ground Black Pepper – to taste

Steps:

1. Preheat the oven to 350°F (180°C).
2. Cut the chicken breasts in half, season with salt and pepper.
3. In a skillet over medium heat, melt the butter and sear the chicken breasts until golden, about 5 minutes on each side.
4. Place the chicken breasts in a baking dish.
5. In the same skillet, sauté the broccoli until tender, about 5 minutes.
6. Arrange the broccoli over the chicken breasts.
7. In a bowl, mix the cream and grated cheese, add finely chopped garlic, salt, and pepper.
8. Pour the creamy cheese sauce over the chicken and broccoli.
9. Bake in the oven for 20 minutes until the cheese melts and the chicken is fully cooked.
10. Serve hot.

5.2 Steak with Garlic Butter

Prep time: 5 minutes
Cook time: 8 minutes
Nutritional Value: 500 kcal per serving | 35 g fats | 40 g proteins | 2 g carbs | 0 g fiber | 300 mg sodium

Ingredients (for 2 servings):

- Steak (beef, ribeye or filet) – 14 oz (400 g)
- Butter – 2 oz (50 g)
- Garlic – 3 cloves
- Rosemary – 1 sprig
- Salt – to taste
- Ground Black Pepper – to taste
- Olive Oil – 1 tbsp

Steps:

1. Heat a skillet over high heat.
2. Rub the steak with olive oil, salt, and pepper.
3. Sear the steak for 3-4 minutes on each side for medium doneness (or to your preference).
4. Remove the steak from the skillet and let it rest.
5. In the same skillet, melt the butter, add finely chopped garlic and rosemary, cook for 1-2 minutes until fragrant.
6. Drizzle the steak with garlic butter before serving.

5.3 Baked Chicken Wings in Spicy Sauce

Prep time: 10 minutes

Cook time: 30 minutes

Nutritional Value: 350 kcal per serving | 25 g fats | 25 g proteins | 3 g carbs | 1 g fiber | 600 mg sodium

Ingredients (for 2 servings):

- Chicken Wings – 17.5 oz (500 g)
- Olive Oil – 2 tbsp
- Soy Sauce (sugar-free) – 2 tbsp
- Garlic – 3 cloves
- Red Pepper (ground) – 1 tsp
- Paprika – 1 tsp
- Lemon Juice – 1 tbsp
- Salt – to taste
- Ground Black Pepper – to taste

Steps:

1. Preheat the oven to 400°F (200°C).
2. In a bowl, mix olive oil, soy sauce, finely chopped garlic, red pepper, paprika, lemon juice, salt, and pepper.
3. Coat the chicken wings in the marinade, mixing well.
4. Arrange the wings on a baking sheet lined with parchment paper.
5. Bake for 25-30 minutes until golden and fully cooked.
6. Serve hot.

5.4 Pork with Cauliflower

Prep time: 10 minutes

Cook time: 20 minutes

Nutritional Value: 400 kcal per serving | 30 g fats | 25 g proteins | 6 g carbs | 2 g fiber | 350 mg sodium

Ingredients (for 2 servings):

- Pork (shoulder or neck) – 10.5 oz (300 g)
- Cauliflower – 7 oz (200 g)
- Onion – 1
- Garlic – 3 cloves
- Butter – 1 oz (30 g)
- Cream (30% fat) – 3.5 oz (100 ml)
- Salt – to taste
- Ground Black Pepper – to taste
- Parsley (fresh, chopped) – for garnish

Steps:

1. Cut the pork into small pieces, season with salt and pepper.
2. Cut the cauliflower into florets, dice the onion, crush and finely chop the garlic.
3. In a skillet, melt the butter and sear the pork until golden, about 5-7 minutes.
4. Add the onion and garlic, cook until the onion is soft, about 3 minutes.
5. Add the cauliflower and cream, cook for 10-12 minutes until the cauliflower is tender and the cream thickens.
6. Season with salt and pepper, sprinkle with chopped parsley before serving.

5.5 Turkey Meatballs with Avocado Sauce

Prep time: 10 minutes

Cook time: 15 minutes

Nutritional Value: 350 kcal per serving | 25 g fats | 20 g proteins | 4 g carbs | 2 g fiber | 300 mg sodium

Ingredients (for 2 servings):

- Turkey (ground) – 10.5 oz (300 g)
- Egg – 1
- Almond Flour – 2 tbsp
- Onion (finely chopped) – 1/2
- Garlic (finely chopped) – 2 cloves
- Parsley (fresh, chopped) – 2 tbsp
- Salt – to taste
- Ground Black Pepper – to taste
- Olive Oil – for frying

For Avocado Sauce:

- Avocado – 1
- Lemon Juice – 1 tbsp
- Cream Cheese – 2 oz (50 g)
- Salt – to taste
- Ground Black Pepper – to taste

Steps:

1. In a bowl, mix turkey, egg, almond flour, onion, garlic, parsley, salt, and pepper until well combined.
2. Form the mixture into small meatballs.
3. In a skillet, heat olive oil and fry the meatballs until golden and fully cooked, about 5-7 minutes on each side.
4. For the avocado sauce, blend the avocado, lemon juice, cream cheese, salt, and pepper until smooth.
5. Serve the meatballs with avocado sauce.

5.6 Pan-Fried Duck with Orange Sauce

Prep time: 10 minutes

Cook time: 15 minutes

Nutritional Value: 450 kcal per serving | 30 g fats | 30 g proteins | 5 g carbs | 0 g fiber | 300 mg sodium

Ingredients (for 2 servings):

- Duck Fillet – 14 oz (400 g)
- Freshly Squeezed Orange Juice – 3.5 oz (100 ml)
- Orange Zest – 1 tsp
- Soy Sauce (sugar-free) – 2 tbsp
- Honey – 1 tsp (optional)
- Garlic – 2 cloves
- Salt – to taste
- Ground Black Pepper – to taste
- Olive Oil – 1 tbsp

Steps:

1. Rub the duck fillet with salt and pepper.
2. Heat a skillet over medium heat and add the olive oil.
3. Sear the duck fillet, skin-side down, until golden, about 5-7 minutes.
4. Turn the fillet and cook for another 5-7 minutes until done.
5. Remove the duck from the skillet and let it rest.
6. In the same skillet, add finely chopped garlic and sauté until fragrant, about 1 minute.
7. Add orange juice, orange zest, soy sauce, and honey (if using), bring to a boil, and cook for 2-3 minutes until the sauce thickens.
8. Drizzle the duck fillet with the orange sauce before serving.

5.7 Chicken Curry with Coconut Milk

Prep time: 10 minutes
Cook time: 20 minutes
Nutritional Value: 350 kcal per serving | 25 g fats | 25 g proteins | 5 g carbs | 2 g fiber | 200 mg sodium

Ingredients (for 2 servings):

- Coconut Milk – 7 oz (200 ml)
- Curry Paste – 2 tbsp
- Onion – 1
- Garlic – 2 cloves
- Fresh Ginger (grated) – 1 tbsp
- Olive Oil – 1 tbsp
- Salt – to taste
- Ground Black Pepper – to taste
- Fresh Cilantro – for garnish

Steps:

1. Cut the chicken breasts into cubes.
2. Finely chop the onion and garlic.
3. In a skillet, heat olive oil and sauté the onion until soft, about 5 minutes.
4. Add garlic and ginger, cook for another 1 minute.
5. Add chicken and curry paste, sauté until golden, about 5-7 minutes.
6. Pour in the coconut milk, season with salt and pepper to taste.
7. Bring to a boil, then reduce heat and simmer for 10-15 minutes until the chicken is cooked through.
8. Serve hot, garnished with fresh cilantro.

5.8 Garlic and Rosemary Baked Ribs

Prep time: 10 minutes
Cook time: 60 minutes
Nutritional Value: 500 kcal per serving | 40 g fats | 30 g proteins | 1 g carbs | 0 g fiber | 400 mg sodium

Ingredients (for 2 servings):

- Pork Ribs – 17.5 oz (500 g)
- Garlic – 4 cloves
- Rosemary – 2 sprigs
- Olive Oil – 2 tbsp
- Salt – to taste
- Ground Black Pepper – to taste

Steps:

1. Preheat the oven to 350°F (180°C).
2. Rub the ribs with salt and pepper.
3. Finely chop the garlic.
4. In a bowl, mix olive oil, garlic, and rosemary.
5. Rub the ribs with the mixture of oil, garlic, and rosemary.
6. Place the ribs on a baking sheet and bake for 45-60 minutes until golden and fully cooked.
7. Serve hot.

5.9 Beef with Mushrooms in Cream Sauce

Prep time: 10 minutes
Cook time: 20 minutes
Nutritional Value: 450 kcal per serving | 35 g fats | 25 g proteins | 5 g carbs | 1 g fiber | 300 mg sodium

Ingredients (for 2 servings):

- Beef (tenderloin or filet) – 10.5 oz (300 g)
- Mushrooms (champignons) – 7 oz (200 g)
- Cream (30% fat) – 5 oz (150 ml)
- Onion – 1
- Garlic – 2 cloves
- Butter – 1 oz (30 g)
- Salt – to taste
- Ground Black Pepper – to taste
- Parsley (fresh, chopped) – for garnish

Steps:

1. Cut the beef into small pieces, season with salt and pepper.
2. Slice the mushrooms, dice the onion, crush and finely chop the garlic.
3. In a skillet, melt the butter and sear the beef until golden, about 5-7 minutes.
4. Add the onion and garlic, cook until the onion is soft, about 3 minutes.
5. Add the mushrooms and cook until golden, about 5-7 minutes.
6. Pour in the cream, bring to a boil, and cook for 5-7 minutes until the sauce thickens.
7. Season with salt and pepper to taste, sprinkle with chopped parsley before serving.

5.10 Baked Turkey with Brussels Sprouts

Prep time: 10 minutes
Cook time: 30 minutes
Nutritional Value: 350 kcal per serving | 25 g fats | 30 g proteins | 6 g carbs | 3 g fiber | 200 mg sodium

Ingredients (for 2 servings):

- Turkey Fillet – 10.5 oz (300 g)
- Brussels Sprouts – 7 oz (200 g)
- Olive Oil – 2 tbsp
- Garlic – 2 cloves
- Salt – to taste
- Ground Black Pepper – to taste
- Lemon Juice – 1 tbsp
- Fresh Thyme – for garnish

Steps:

1. Preheat the oven to 350°F (180°C).
2. Cut the turkey fillet into portions, season with salt and pepper.
3. Halve the Brussels sprouts.
4. In a bowl, mix olive oil, finely chopped garlic, and lemon juice.
5. Place the turkey and Brussels sprouts on a baking sheet, drizzle with the garlic and lemon oil.
6. Bake for 25-30 minutes until golden and the turkey is fully cooked.
7. Serve hot, garnished with fresh thyme.

5.11 Chicken Skewers with Green Vegetables

Prep time: **30 minutes**
Cook time: **12 minutes**

Nutritional Value:
300 kcal per serving | 20 g fats | 25 g proteins | 6 g carbs | 2 g fiber | 200 mg sodium

Ingredients (for 2 servings):

- Chicken Breasts – 300 g
- Zucchini – 1
- Green Bell Pepper – 1
- Olive Oil – 2 tbsp
- Lemon Juice – 1 tbsp
- Garlic – 2 cloves
- Salt – to taste
- Ground Black Pepper – to taste
- Fresh Thyme – for garnish

Steps:

1. Cut the chicken breasts and zucchini into cubes, and the green bell pepper into strips.
2. In a bowl, mix olive oil, lemon juice, finely chopped garlic, salt, and pepper.
3. Marinate the chicken and vegetables in this mixture for 30 minutes.
4. Thread the chicken and vegetables onto skewers, alternating them.
5. Preheat the grill to medium heat and cook the skewers for 10-12 minutes, turning every few minutes, until the chicken is fully cooked.
6. Serve hot, garnished with fresh thyme.

5.12 Spiced Baked Ham

Prep time: **10 minutes**
Cook time: **90 minutes**

Nutritional Value:
450 kcal per serving | 35 g fats | 30 g proteins | 2 g carbs | 0 g fiber | 300 mg sodium

Ingredients (for 2 servings):

- Pork (tenderloin or ham) – 500 g
- Garlic – 4 cloves
- Mustard – 2 tbsp
- Olive Oil – 2 tbsp
- Dried Rosemary – 1 tsp
- Dried Thyme – 1 tsp
- Salt – to taste
- Ground Black Pepper – to taste

Steps:

1. Preheat the oven to 350°F (180°C).
2. Rub the pork with salt, pepper, rosemary, and thyme.
3. Finely chop the garlic and mix it with mustard and olive oil.
4. Rub the pork with this mixture.
5. Place the pork in a baking dish and bake for 1.5-2 hours until fully cooked.
6. Let the ham rest before slicing into serving pieces.

5.13 Beef Rolls Stuffed with Spinach and Cheese

Prep time: 10 minutes
Cook time: 25 minutes
Nutritional Value: 350 kcal per serving | 20 g fats | 30 g proteins | 3 g carbs | 1 g fiber | 250 mg sodium

Ingredients (for 2 servings):

- Beef (thinly sliced) – 300 g
- Fresh Spinach – 100 g
- Cheese (mozzarella, grated) – 50 g
- Garlic – 2 cloves
- Olive Oil – 1 tbsp
- Salt – to taste
- Ground Black Pepper – to taste

Steps:

1. Preheat the oven to 350°F (180°C).
2. In a skillet, heat olive oil and sauté finely chopped garlic until fragrant, about 1 minute.
3. Add spinach and cook until wilted, about 3 minutes.
4. Place some spinach and grated cheese on each beef slice and roll up.
5. Secure the rolls with toothpicks and place them in a baking dish.
6. Bake for 20-25 minutes until fully cooked.
7. Serve hot.

5.14 Chicken and Avocado Burger

Prep time: 10 minutes
Cook time: 15 minutes
Nutritional Value: 400 kcal per serving | 25 g fats | 30 g proteins | 6 g carbs | 3 g fiber | 300 mg sodium

Ingredients (for 2 servings):

- Chicken Breasts (minced) – 300 g
- Avocado – 1
- Lettuce Leaves – 4
- Tomato – 1
- Red Onion – 1/2
- Cheese (cheddar, slices) – 2
- Olive Oil – 1 tbsp
- Mayonnaise (keto) – 2 tbsp
- Salt – to taste
- Ground Black Pepper – to taste

Steps:

1. Form patties from the minced chicken, season with salt and pepper.
2. Heat a skillet over medium heat and fry the patties in olive oil for 5-7 minutes on each side until fully cooked.
3. Slice the avocado, tomato, and red onion thinly.
4. Assemble the burger: place a patty on a lettuce leaf, top with cheese, avocado slices, tomato, and red onion, add mayonnaise, and cover with another lettuce leaf.
5. Serve immediately.

6. SIDE DISHES

6.1 Cauliflower Rice

Prep time: 10 minutes
Cook time: 7 minutes
Nutritional Value: 100 kcal per serving | 7 g fats | 2 g proteins | 7 g carbs | 3 g fiber | 150 mg sodium

Ingredients (for 2 servings):

- Cauliflower – 400 g
- Olive Oil – 2 tbsp
- Salt – to taste
- Ground Black Pepper – to taste

Steps:

1. Break the cauliflower into florets and grate them on a large grater or process in a food processor until they resemble rice.
2. Heat the olive oil in a large skillet over medium heat.
3. Add the cauliflower and cook, stirring, for about 5-7 minutes until soft.
4. Season with salt and pepper to taste.
5. Serve hot.

6.2 Zucchini Noodles with Garlic

Prep time: 10 minutes
Cook time: 5 minutes
Nutritional Value: 150 kcal per serving | 10 g fats | 2 g proteins | 8 g carbs | 2 g fiber | 200 mg sodium

Ingredients (for 2 servings):

- Zucchini – 2
- Garlic – 2 cloves
- Olive Oil – 2 tbsp
- Salt – to taste
- Ground Black Pepper – to taste
- Fresh Herbs (for garnish) – to taste

Steps:

1. Slice the zucchini into thin strips using a vegetable peeler.
2. Finely chop the garlic.
3. Heat the olive oil in a large skillet over medium heat.
4. Add the garlic and cook until fragrant, about 1 minute.
5. Add the zucchini noodles and cook, stirring, for about 3-5 minutes until soft.
6. Season with salt and pepper to taste.
7. Serve garnished with fresh herbs.

6.3 Almond Flour Bread

Prep time: 10 minutes
Cook time: 30 minutes
Nutritional Value: 300 kcal per serving | 25 g fats | 10 g proteins | 5 g carbs | 3 g fiber | 200 mg sodium

Ingredients (for 2 servings):

- Almond Flour – 100 g
- Eggs – 2
- Butter (melted) – 2 tbsp
- Baking Powder – 1 tsp
- Salt – a pinch
- Sweetener (optional) – to taste

Steps:

1. Preheat the oven to 350°F (180°C).
2. In a large bowl, beat the eggs.
3. Add almond flour, baking powder, salt, and melted butter, mixing until smooth.
4. Pour the batter into a greased baking dish.
5. Bake in the oven for about 25-30 minutes until golden brown.
6. Let the bread cool before slicing.

6.4 Cauliflower Mashed Potatoes

Prep time: 5 minutes
Cook time: 15 minutes
Nutritional Value: 200 kcal per serving | 18 g fats | 3 g proteins | 7 g carbs | 3 g fiber | 150 mg sodium

Ingredients (for 2 servings):

- Cauliflower – 400 g
- Butter – 2 tbsp
- Heavy Cream (30% fat) – 50 ml
- Salt – to taste
- Ground Black Pepper – to taste
- Fresh Herbs (for garnish) – to taste

Steps:

1. Break the cauliflower into florets and boil in salted water until tender, about 10 minutes.
2. Drain and let the cauliflower cool slightly.
3. In a food processor or blender, puree the cauliflower until smooth.
4. Add butter and cream, blending until smooth.
5. Season with salt and pepper to taste.
6. Serve garnished with fresh herbs.

6.5 Roasted Brussels Sprouts

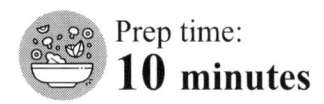

Prep time: 10 minutes

Cook time: 25 minutes

Nutritional Value: 200 kcal per serving | 15 g fats | 5 g proteins | 12 g carbs | 6 g fiber | 150 mg sodium

Ingredients (for 2 servings):

- Brussels Sprouts – 400 g
- Olive Oil – 2 tbsp
- Garlic – 2 cloves
- Salt – to taste
- Ground Black Pepper – to taste

Steps:

1. Preheat the oven to 400°F (200°C).
2. Cut the Brussels sprouts in half.
3. Crush and finely chop the garlic.
4. In a large bowl, mix the Brussels sprouts, olive oil, garlic, salt, and pepper.
5. Spread the Brussels sprouts on a baking sheet in a single layer.
6. Roast in the oven for 20-25 minutes until golden brown.
7. Serve hot.

6.6 Grilled Mushrooms

Prep time: 35 minutes

Cook time: 10 minutes

Nutritional Value: 180 kcal per serving | 14 g fats | 6 g proteins | 6 g carbs | 2 g fiber | 120 mg sodium

Ingredients (for 2 servings):

- Mushrooms or Portobello – 400 g
- Olive Oil – 2 tbsp
- Garlic – 2 cloves
- Lemon Juice – 1 tbsp
- Salt – to taste
- Ground Black Pepper – to taste
- Fresh Herbs (for garnish) – to taste

Steps:

1. Clean the mushrooms and remove the stems.
2. Crush and finely chop the garlic.
3. In a large bowl, mix the olive oil, lemon juice, garlic, salt, and pepper.
4. Marinate the mushrooms in this mixture for 15 minutes.
5. Preheat the grill to medium temperature.
6. Grill the mushrooms for 3-5 minutes on each side until tender.
7. Serve garnished with fresh herbs.

6.7 Spinach and Walnut Salad

Prep time: 10 minutes
Cook time: 5 minutes

Nutritional Value:
250 kcal per serving | 20 g fats | 5 g proteins | 8 g carbs | 4 g fiber | 150 mg sodium

Ingredients (for 2 servings):

- Fresh Spinach – 100 g
- Walnuts – 50 g
- Red Onion – 1/2
- Olive Oil – 2 tbsp
- Lemon Juice – 1 tbsp
- Salt – to taste
- Ground Black Pepper – to taste

Steps:

1. Wash and dry the spinach.
2. Slice the red onion into thin rings.
3. In a large bowl, mix the spinach, walnuts, and red onion.
4. In a separate bowl, mix the olive oil, lemon juice, salt, and pepper.
5. Pour the dressing over the salad and toss well.
6. Serve immediately.

6.8 Grilled Eggplant with Garlic

Prep time: 25 minutes
Cook time: 10 minutes

Nutritional Value:
200 kcal per serving | 15 g fats | 2 g proteins | 15 g carbs | 7 g fiber | 120 mg sodium

Ingredients (for 2 servings):

- Eggplants – 2
- Olive Oil – 2 tbsp
- Garlic – 2 cloves
- Lemon Juice – 1 tbsp
- Salt – to taste
- Ground Black Pepper – to taste
- Fresh Herbs (for garnish) – to taste

Steps:

1. Slice the eggplants into 1 cm thick rounds.
2. Crush and finely chop the garlic.
3. In a large bowl, mix the olive oil, lemon juice, garlic, salt, and pepper.
4. Marinate the eggplant slices in this mixture for 15 minutes.
5. Preheat the grill to medium temperature.
6. Grill the eggplant slices for 3-5 minutes on each side until tender.
7. Serve garnished with fresh herbs.

6.9 Radish "Potatoes"

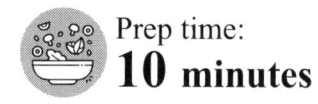

Prep time: 10 minutes
Cook time: 15 minutes

Nutritional Value:
150 kcal per serving | 10 g fats | 2 g proteins | 10 g carbs | 3 g fiber | 150 mg sodium

Ingredients (for 2 servings):

- Radishes – 400 g
- Olive Oil – 2 tbsp
- Garlic – 2 cloves
- Salt – to taste
- Ground Black Pepper – to taste
- Fresh Herbs (for garnish) – to taste

Steps:

1. Peel and dice the radishes.
2. Crush and finely chop the garlic.
3. Heat the olive oil in a large skillet over medium heat.
4. Add the diced radishes and cook, stirring, for about 10-15 minutes until golden brown.
5. Add the garlic and cook for another 1-2 minutes.
6. Season with salt and pepper to taste.
7. Serve garnished with fresh herbs.

6.10 Green Beans with Bacon

Prep time: 5 minutes
Cook time: 10 minutes

Nutritional Value:
200 kcal per serving | 15 g fats | 7 g proteins | 8 g carbs | 4 g fiber | 400 mg sodium

Ingredients (for 2 servings):

- Green Beans – 300 g
- Bacon – 100 g
- Garlic – 2 cloves
- Olive Oil – 1 tbsp
- Salt – to taste
- Ground Black Pepper – to taste

Steps:

1. Cut the bacon into small pieces.
2. Heat the olive oil in a large skillet over medium heat.
3. Fry the bacon until golden brown, then add the finely chopped garlic and cook for another 1 minute.
4. Add the green beans and cook, stirring, for about 5-7 minutes until tender.
5. Season with salt and pepper to taste.
6. Serve hot.

6.11 Fried Zucchini with Cheese

Prep time: 10 minutes

Cook time: 10 minutes

Nutritional Value: 250 kcal per serving | 20 g fats | 7 g proteins | 6 g carbs | 2 g fiber | 300 mg sodium

Ingredients (for 2 servings):

- Zucchini – 2
- Parmesan cheese (grated) – 50 g
- Olive Oil – 2 tbsp
- Garlic – 2 cloves
- Salt – to taste
- Ground Black Pepper – to taste
- Fresh Herbs (for garnish) – to taste

Steps:

1. Slice the zucchini into rounds.
2. Crush and finely chop the garlic.
3. Heat the olive oil in a large skillet over medium heat.
4. Add the sliced zucchini and cook, stirring, for about 5-7 minutes until tender and golden brown.
5. Add the garlic and cook for another 1-2 minutes.
6. Sprinkle with grated cheese and cook until the cheese melts.
7. Season with salt and pepper to taste.
8. Serve garnished with fresh herbs.

6.12 Flaxseed Crackers

Prep time: 10 minutes

Cook time: 30 minutes

Nutritional Value: 250 kcal per serving | 20 g fats | 7 g proteins | 4 g carbs | 6 g fiber | 150 mg sodium

Ingredients (for 2 servings):

- Flaxseeds – 100 g
- Water – 200 ml
- Salt – to taste
- Garlic powder – 1/2 tsp (optional)
- Italian herbs – 1/2 tsp (optional)

Steps:

1. Preheat the oven to 350°F (180°C).
2. In a bowl, mix the flaxseeds, water, salt, garlic powder, and Italian herbs.
3. Let the mixture sit for 10 minutes to allow the seeds to swell.
4. Spread the mixture thinly on a baking sheet lined with parchment paper.
5. Bake in the oven for about 30 minutes until golden brown.
6. Let the crackers cool completely before breaking them into pieces.

6.13 Cabbage Salad with Avocado

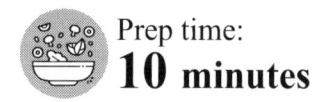

Prep time: 10 minutes

Cook time: 5 minutes

Nutritional Value:
250 kcal per serving | 20 g fats | 3 g proteins | 10 g carbs | 5 g fiber | 200 mg sodium

Ingredients (for 2 servings):

- White cabbage – 300 g
- Avocado – 1
- Fresh cucumber – 1
- Green onion – 30 g
- Olive Oil – 2 tbsp
- Lemon Juice – 1 tbsp
- Salt – to taste
- Ground Black Pepper – to taste

Steps:

1. Shred the cabbage into thin strips.
2. Dice the avocado and cucumber.
3. Finely chop the green onion.
4. In a large bowl, mix the cabbage, avocado, cucumber, and green onion.
5. Drizzle with olive oil and lemon juice, season with salt and pepper.
6. Toss well and serve immediately.8. Serve garnished with fresh herbs.

6.14 Baked Sweet Peppers

Prep time: 5 minutes

Cook time: 25 minutes

Nutritional Value:
150 kcal per serving | 10 g fats | 2 g proteins | 12 g carbs | 4 g fiber | 150 mg sodium

Ingredients (for 2 servings):

- Sweet peppers – 4
- Olive Oil – 2 tbsp
- Garlic – 2 cloves
- Salt – to taste
- Ground Black Pepper – to taste
- Fresh Herbs (for garnish) – to taste

Steps:

1. Preheat the oven to 400°F (200°C).
2. Cut the sweet peppers in half and remove the seeds.
3. Crush and finely chop the garlic.
4. Place the peppers on a baking sheet, drizzle with olive oil, sprinkle with garlic, salt, and pepper.
5. Bake in the oven for 20-25 minutes until tender and golden brown.
6. Serve hot, garnished with fresh herbs.

7. SAUCES AND DRESSINGS

7.1 Mayonnaise

Prep time: **5 minutes**

Cook time: **5 minutes**

Nutritional Value:
200 kcal per serving | 22 g fats | 1 g proteins | 0 g carbs | 0 g fiber | 150 mg sodium

Ingredients (for 2 servings):

- Egg yolk – 1
- Mustard – 1 tsp
- Lemon juice – 1 tbsp
- Olive oil – 100 ml
- Salt – to taste
- Ground Black Pepper – to taste

Steps:

1. In a bowl, mix the egg yolk, mustard, and lemon juice.
2. Gradually add the olive oil, whisking continuously until thick.
3. Season with salt and pepper to taste.
4. Store in the refrigerator until serving.

7.2 Caesar Dressing

Prep time: **5 minutes**

Cook time: **5 minutes**

Nutritional Value:
250 kcal per serving | 25 g fats | 4 g proteins | 1 g carbs | 0 g fiber | 200 mg sodium

Ingredients (for 2 servings):

- Egg yolk – 1
- Garlic – 1 clove
- Anchovies – 2
- Lemon juice – 1 tbsp
- Worcestershire sauce – 1 tsp
- Mustard – 1 tsp
- Olive oil – 50 ml
- Parmesan cheese (grated) – 2 tbsp
- Salt – to taste
- Ground Black Pepper – to taste

Steps:

1. In a blender, combine the egg yolk, garlic, anchovies, lemon juice, Worcestershire sauce, and mustard.
2. Gradually add the olive oil while blending until smooth.
3. Add grated Parmesan, salt, and pepper, and blend until combined.
4. Store in the refrigerator until serving.

7.3 Pesto

Prep time: **5 minutes**

Cook time: **5 minutes**

Nutritional Value:
300 kcal per serving | 28 g fats | 5 g proteins | 3 g carbs | 1 g fiber | 150 mg sodium

Ingredients (for 2 servings):

- Fresh basil – 50 g
- Pine nuts – 30 g
- Garlic – 2 cloves
- Parmesan cheese (grated) – 30 g
- Olive oil – 50 ml
- Salt – to taste
- Ground Black Pepper – to taste

Steps:

1. In a blender, combine basil, pine nuts, garlic, and Parmesan.
2. Gradually add olive oil while blending until smooth.
3. Season with salt and pepper to taste.
4. Store in the refrigerator until serving.

7.4 Creamy Garlic Sauce

Prep time: **5 minutes**

Cook time: **10 minutes**

Nutritional Value:
350 kcal per serving | 33 g fats | 5 g proteins | 2 g carbs | 0 g fiber | 200 mg sodium

Ingredients (for 2 servings):

- Cream (30% fat) – 200 ml
- Garlic – 2 cloves
- Butter – 1 tbsp
- Parmesan cheese (grated) – 30 g
- Salt – to taste
- Ground Black Pepper – to taste

Steps:

1. Crush and finely chop the garlic.
2. Melt the butter in a skillet over medium heat.
3. Add the garlic and cook until fragrant, about 1-2 minutes.
4. Add the cream and grated Parmesan, stirring constantly.
5. Simmer on low heat until thickened, about 5-7 minutes.
6. Season with salt and pepper to taste.
7. Serve hot.

7.5 Guacamole

Prep time: **10 minutes**

Cook time: **5 minutes**

Nutritional Value:
250 kcal per serving | 23 g fats | 3 g proteins | 12 g carbs | 9 g fiber | 150 mg sodium

Ingredients (for 2 servings):

- Avocado – 2
- Lime – 1
- Tomato – 1
- Red onion – 1/2
- Garlic – 1 clove
- Fresh cilantro – 20 g
- Salt – to taste
- Ground Black Pepper – to taste

Steps:

1. Mash the avocado flesh in a bowl.
2. Squeeze the lime juice and add it to the avocado.
3. Finely dice the tomato, red onion, and garlic.
4. Mix the avocado with the diced vegetables.
5. Add finely chopped cilantro, salt, and pepper to taste.
6. Mix thoroughly and serve immediately.

7.6 Garlic Sauce

Prep time: **5 minutes**

Cook time: **5 minutes**

Nutritional Value:
200 kcal per serving | 22 g fats | 1 g proteins | 1 g carbs | 0 g fiber | 150 mg sodium

Ingredients (for 2 servings):

- Keto mayonnaise – 100 g
- Garlic – 3 cloves
- Lemon juice – 1 tbsp
- Salt – to taste
- Ground Black Pepper – to taste

Steps:

1. Crush and finely chop the garlic.
2. In a bowl, mix the mayonnaise, lemon juice, garlic, salt, and pepper.
3. Stir well and store in the refrigerator until serving.

7.7 Tartar Sauce

Prep time: **5 minutes**

Cook time: **5 minutes**

Nutritional Value:
220 kcal per serving | 24 g fats | 2 g proteins | 2 g carbs | 0 g fiber | 200 mg sodium

Ingredients (for 2 servings):

- Keto mayonnaise – 100 g
- Pickles – 50 g
- Capers – 1 tbsp
- Lemon juice – 1 tbsp
- Salt – to taste
- Ground Black Pepper – to taste

Steps:

1. Finely chop the pickles and capers.
2. In a bowl, mix the mayonnaise, lemon juice, chopped pickles, and capers.
3. Season with salt and pepper to taste.
4. Stir well and store in the refrigerator until serving.

7.8 Alfredo Sauce

Prep time: **5 minutes**

Cook time: **10 minutes**

Nutritional Value:
350 kcal per serving | 33 g fats | 6 g proteins | 2 g carbs | 0 g fiber | 200 mg sodium

Ingredients (for 2 servings):

- Cream (30% fat) – 200 ml
- Butter – 2 tbsp
- Garlic – 2 cloves
- Parmesan cheese (grated) – 50 g
- Salt – to taste
- Ground Black Pepper – to taste

Steps:

1. Crush and finely chop the garlic.
2. Melt the butter in a skillet over medium heat.
3. Add the garlic and cook until fragrant, about 1-2 minutes.
4. Add the cream and grated Parmesan, stirring constantly.
5. Simmer on low heat until thickened, about 5-7 minutes.
6. Season with salt and pepper to taste.
7. Serve hot.

7.9 Barbecue Sauce

Prep time: **5 minutes**
Cook time: **10 minutes**

Nutritional Value:
50 kcal per serving | 0 g fats | 2 g proteins | 8 g carbs | 2 g fiber | 300 mg sodium

Ingredients (for 2 servings):

- Tomato paste – 100 g
- Apple cider vinegar – 2 tbsp
- Worcestershire sauce – 1 tbsp
- Sweetener (erythritol) – 1 tbsp
- Smoked paprika – 1 tsp
- Garlic powder – 1 tsp
- Onion powder – 1 tsp
- Salt – to taste
- Ground Black Pepper – to taste

Steps:

1. In a bowl, mix all the ingredients until smooth.
2. Pour the mixture into a saucepan and bring to a boil over medium heat.
3. Reduce heat and simmer, stirring occasionally, for about 10 minutes.
4. Let the sauce cool before serving.

7.10 Marinara Sauce

Prep time: **5 minutes**
Cook time: **20 minutes**

Nutritional Value:
100 kcal per serving | 7 g fats | 2 g proteins | 8 g carbs | 2 g fiber | 200 mg sodium

Ingredients (for 2 servings):

- Tomato paste – 200 g
- Olive oil – 2 tbsp
- Garlic – 3 cloves
- Onion – 1
- Italian herbs – 1 tsp
- Salt – to taste
- Ground Black Pepper – to taste

Steps:

1. Finely chop the onion and garlic.
2. Heat the olive oil in a skillet over medium heat.
3. Add the onion and garlic, cook until soft, about 5 minutes.
4. Add the tomato paste and Italian herbs, bring to a boil.
5. Reduce heat and simmer the sauce for about 15 minutes, stirring occasionally.
6. Season with salt and pepper to taste.
7. Serve hot or cold.

7.11 Hollandaise Sauce

Prep time: 5 minutes

Cook time: 10 minutes

Nutritional Value: 200 kcal per serving | 22 g fats | 2 g proteins | 1 g carbs | 0 g fiber | 150 mg sodium

Ingredients (for 2 servings):

- Egg yolks – 2
- Lemon juice – 1 tbsp
- Water – 1 tbsp
- Butter – 100 g
- Salt – to taste
- Ground Black Pepper – to taste

Steps:

1. In a bowl, whisk the egg yolks with lemon juice and water.
2. Melt the butter over medium heat.
3. Gradually add the melted butter to the egg yolks, whisking constantly until thickened.
4. Add salt and pepper to taste.
5. Serve immediately.

7.12 Ranch Dressing

Prep time: 5 minutes

Cook time: 5 minutes

Nutritional Value: 250 kcal per serving | 25 g fats | 2 g proteins | 2 g carbs | 0 g fiber | 200 mg sodium

Ingredients (for 2 servings):

- Keto mayonnaise – 100 g
- Sour cream (20% fat) – 50 g
- Garlic powder – 1/2 tsp
- Onion powder – 1/2 tsp
- Dried dill – 1 tsp
- Dried parsley – 1 tsp
- Lemon juice – 1 tbsp
- Salt – to taste
- Ground Black Pepper – to taste

Steps:

1. In a bowl, mix the mayonnaise, sour cream, garlic powder, onion powder, dill, and parsley.
2. Add lemon juice, salt, and pepper to taste.
3. Mix well until smooth.
4. Store in the refrigerator until serving.

7.13 Salsa

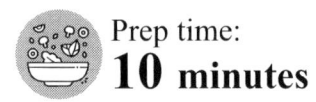

Prep time: 10 minutes

Cook time: 5 minutes

Nutritional Value: 40 kcal per serving | 1 g fats | 2 g proteins | 8 g carbs | 2 g fiber | 150 mg sodium

Ingredients (for 2 servings):

- Tomatoes – 3
- Red onion – 1/2
- Chili pepper – 1 (optional)
- Garlic – 2 cloves
- Lime juice – 1 tbsp
- Fresh cilantro – 20 g
- Salt – to taste
- Ground Black Pepper – to taste

Steps:

1. Finely chop the tomatoes, red onion, and chili pepper.
2. Crush and finely chop the garlic.
3. Finely chop the cilantro.
4. In a large bowl, mix the chopped vegetables, garlic, and cilantro.
5. Add lime juice, salt, and pepper to taste.
6. Mix thoroughly and serve immediately.

7.14 Creamy Cheese Sauce

Prep time: 5 minutes

Cook time: 10 minutes

Nutritional Value: 350 kcal per serving | 33 g fats | 8 g proteins | 2 g carbs | 0 g fiber | 200 mg sodium

Ingredients (for 2 servings):

- Cream (30% fat) – 200 ml
- Butter – 2 tbsp
- Cheddar cheese (grated) – 100 g
- Garlic – 1 clove
- Salt – to taste
- Ground Black Pepper – to taste

Steps:

1. Crush and finely chop the garlic.
2. Melt the butter in a skillet over medium heat.
3. Add the garlic and cook until fragrant, about 1-2 minutes.
4. Add the cream and grated Cheddar, stirring constantly.
5. Simmer on low heat until thickened, about 5-7 minutes.
6. Season with salt and pepper to taste.
7. Serve hot.

8. DESSERTS

8.1 Chocolate Cake

Prep time: 15 minutes
Cook time: 30 minutes
Nutritional Value: 350 kcal per serving | 30 g fats | 8 g proteins | 10 g carbs | 5 g fiber | 200 mg sodium

Ingredients (for 2 servings):

- Almond flour – 100 g
- Cocoa powder – 50 g
- Baking powder – 1 tsp
- Eggs – 2
- Erythritol – 100 g
- Butter (melted) – 100 g
- Vanilla extract – 1 tsp
- Cream (30% fat) – 100 ml

Steps:

1. Preheat the oven to 350°F (180°C).
2. In a bowl, mix almond flour, cocoa powder, and baking powder.
3. In another bowl, beat the eggs with erythritol until fluffy.
4. Add the melted butter and vanilla extract to the eggs and mix well.
5. Gradually add the dry ingredients to the liquid mixture, stirring until smooth.
6. Pour in the cream and mix.
7. Pour the batter into a greased baking dish.
8. Bake for 25-30 minutes until done.
9. Allow the cake to cool before serving.

8.2 Cheesecake

Prep time: 15 minutes
Cook time: 30 minutes
Nutritional Value: 400 kcal per serving | 35 g fats | 8 g proteins | 6 g carbs | 2 g fiber | 300 mg sodium

Ingredients (for 2 servings):

For the crust:
- Almond flour – 50 g
- Butter (melted) – 2 tbsp
- Erythritol – 1 tbsp

For the filling:
- Cream cheese – 200 g
- Cream (30% fat) – 100 ml
- Egg – 1
- Erythritol – 50 g
- Vanilla extract – 1 tsp

Steps:

1. Preheat the oven to 356°F (180°C).
2. In a bowl, mix almond flour, melted butter, and erythritol for the crust.
3. Press the mixture into a baking dish.
4. Bake the crust for 10 minutes, then let it cool.
5. In a bowl, beat the cream cheese, cream, egg, erythritol, and vanilla extract until smooth.
6. Pour the filling over the cooled crust.
7. Bake the cheesecake for 25-30 minutes until lightly golden.
8. Allow the cheesecake to cool before serving.

8.3 Avocado Ice Cream

Prep time: 10 minutes

Cook time: 2-3 hours (freezing)

Nutritional Value: 300 kcal per serving | 28 g fats | 4 g proteins | 8 g carbs | 5 g fiber | 100 mg sodium

Ingredients (for 2 servings):

- Avocados – 2
- Cream (30% fat) – 200 ml
- Erythritol – 50 g
- Lemon juice – 1 tbsp
- Vanilla extract – 1 tsp

Steps:

1. In a blender, mix avocado flesh, cream, erythritol, lemon juice, and vanilla extract until smooth.
2. Transfer the mixture to a container and freeze for 2-3 hours.
3. Stir the ice cream with a fork every 30 minutes to prevent ice crystals from forming.
4. Serve frozen.

8.4 Almond Flour Cookies

Prep time: 10 minutes

Cook time: 12 minutes

Nutritional Value: 250 kcal per serving | 20 g fats | 6 g proteins | 5 g carbs | 3 g fiber | 150 mg sodium

Ingredients (for 2 servings):

- Almond flour – 100 g
- Erythritol – 50 g
- Butter (melted) – 50 g
- Egg – 1
- Vanilla extract – 1 tsp
- Baking powder – 1/2 tsp

Steps:

1. Preheat the oven to 356°F (180°C).
2. In a bowl, mix almond flour, erythritol, and baking powder.
3. In another bowl, beat the egg, add the melted butter and vanilla extract, and mix well.
4. Gradually add the dry ingredients to the liquid mixture, stirring until smooth.
5. Form small balls from the dough and place them on a baking sheet lined with parchment paper.
6. Bake the cookies for 10-12 minutes until golden.
7. Allow the cookies to cool before serving.

8.5 Brownies

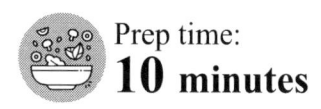

Prep time: 10 minutes

Cook time: 25 minutes

Nutritional Value: 300 kcal per serving | 25 g fats | 6 g proteins | 8 g carbs | 4 g fiber | 150 mg sodium

Ingredients (for 2 servings):

- Almond flour – 50 g
- Cocoa powder – 30 g
- Erythritol – 50 g
- Butter (melted) – 50 g
- Egg – 1
- Vanilla extract – 1 tsp
- Baking powder – 1/2 tsp
- Salt – a pinch

Steps:

1. Preheat the oven to 356°F (180°C).
2. In a bowl, mix almond flour, cocoa powder, erythritol, baking powder, and salt.
3. In another bowl, beat the egg, add the melted butter and vanilla extract, and mix well.
4. Gradually add the dry ingredients to the liquid mixture, stirring until smooth.
5. Pour the batter into a greased baking dish.
6. Bake for 20-25 minutes until done.
7. Allow the brownies to cool before cutting and serving.

8.6 Lemon Cupcakes

Prep time: 10 minutes

Cook time: 25 minutes

Nutritional Value: 300 kcal per serving | 25 g fats | 8 g proteins | 5 g carbs | 3 g fiber | 150 mg sodium

Ingredients (for 2 servings):

- Almond flour – 100 g
- Eggs – 2
- Butter (melted) – 50 g
- Erythritol – 50 g
- Lemon juice – 2 tbsp
- Lemon zest – 1 tsp
- Baking powder – 1 tsp
- Vanilla extract – 1 tsp

Steps:

1. Preheat the oven to 356°F (180°C).
2. In a bowl, beat the eggs with erythritol until fluffy.
3. Add melted butter, lemon juice, lemon zest, and vanilla extract, and mix well.
4. In another bowl, mix almond flour and baking powder.
5. Gradually add the dry ingredients to the liquid mixture, stirring until smooth.
6. Pour the batter into cupcake molds.
7. Bake for 20-25 minutes until golden brown.
8. Allow the cupcakes to cool before serving.

8.7 Apple Pie

Prep time: 15 minutes

Cook time: 30 minutes

Nutritional Value:
350 kcal per serving | 28 g fats | 6 g proteins | 12 g carbs | 4 g fiber | 200 mg sodium

Ingredients (for 2 servings):

For the crust:
- Almond flour – 100 g
- Butter (melted) – 2 tbsp
- Erythritol – 1 tbsp

For the filling:
- Apple – 1
- Cinnamon – 1 tsp
- Erythritol – 2 tbsp
- Butter – 1 tbsp

Steps:

1. Preheat the oven to 356°F (180°C).
2. In a bowl, mix almond flour, melted butter, and erythritol for the crust.
3. Press the mixture into a baking dish.
4. Bake the crust for 10 minutes, then let it cool.
5. Slice the apple thinly.
6. In a skillet, melt butter, add sliced apple, cinnamon, and erythritol. Cook until the apples are soft, about 5-7 minutes.
7. Spread the filling over the cooled crust.
8. Bake the pie for 15-20 minutes until golden brown.
9. Allow the pie to cool before serving.

8.8 Coconut Candies

Prep time: 10 minutes

Cook time: 1 hour (chilling)

Nutritional Value:
250 kcal per serving | 22 g fats | 2 g proteins | 6 g carbs | 4 g fiber | 100 mg sodium

Ingredients (for 2 servings):

- Shredded coconut – 100 g
- Butter (melted) – 50 g
- Erythritol – 2 tbsp
- Coconut milk – 2 tbsp
- Vanilla extract – 1 tsp

Steps:

1. In a bowl, mix shredded coconut, melted butter, erythritol, coconut milk, and vanilla extract.
2. Form small balls from the mixture.
3. Place the candies on a baking sheet lined with parchment paper.
4. Chill in the refrigerator for at least 1 hour before serving.

8.9 Coconut Truffles

Prep time: 10 minutes

Cook time: 1 hour (chilling)

Nutritional Value: 300 kcal per serving | 25 g fats | 3 g proteins | 8 g carbs | 5 g fiber | 150 mg sodium

Ingredients (for 2 servings):

- Shredded coconut – 100 g
- Cream (30% fat) – 50 ml
- Erythritol – 2 tbsp
- Cocoa powder – 2 tbsp
- Vanilla extract – 1 tsp

Steps:

1. In a bowl, mix shredded coconut, cream, erythritol, and vanilla extract.
2. Form small balls from the mixture.
3. Roll each ball in cocoa powder.
4. Place the truffles on a baking sheet lined with parchment paper.
5. Chill in the refrigerator for at least 1 hour before serving.

8.10 Marshmallows

Prep time: 10 minutes

Cook time: 15 minutes (not including setting time)

Nutritional Value: 50 kcal per serving | 0 g fats | 1 g proteins | 13 g carbs | 0 g fiber | 20 mg sodium

Ingredients (for 2 servings):

- Gelatin – 1 packet (10 g)
- Water – 100 ml
- Erythritol – 100 g
- Vanilla extract – 1 tsp
- Lemon juice – 1 tbsp
- Salt – a pinch

Steps:

1. In a small saucepan, mix gelatin with 50 ml of water and let it sit for 5 minutes.
2. In another saucepan, mix erythritol and the remaining 50 ml of water. Bring to a boil and cook over medium heat until the erythritol is fully dissolved.
3. Add lemon juice, salt, and vanilla extract to the erythritol mixture.
4. Pour the hot mixture into the gelatin and beat with a mixer on high speed until fluffy, about 10-15 minutes.
5. Pour the mixture into a mold lined with parchment paper and let it set for 2-3 hours.
6. Cut the marshmallows into pieces before serving.

8.11 Cocoa Truffles

Prep time: 10 minutes
Cook time: 1 hour (chilling)
Nutritional Value: 300 kcal per serving | 25 g fats | 3 g proteins | 8 g carbs | 5 g fiber | 150 mg sodium

Ingredients (for 2 servings):

- Shredded coconut – 100 g
- Cream (30% fat) – 50 ml
- Erythritol – 2 tbsp
- Cocoa powder – 3 tbsp
- Vanilla extract – 1 tsp

Steps:

1. In a bowl, mix shredded coconut, cream, erythritol, and vanilla extract.
2. Form small balls from the mixture.
3. Roll each ball in cocoa powder.
4. Place the truffles on a baking sheet lined with parchment paper.
5. Chill in the refrigerator for at least 1 hour before serving.

8.12 Nut Cookies

Prep time: 10 minutes
Cook time: 12 minutes
Nutritional Value: 300 kcal per serving | 25 g fats | 7 g proteins | 6 g carbs | 3 g fiber | 150 mg sodium

Ingredients (for 2 servings):

- Almond flour – 100 g
- Nuts (walnuts or almonds) – 50 g
- Erythritol – 50 g
- Butter (melted) – 50 g
- Egg – 1
- Vanilla extract – 1 tsp
- Baking powder – 1/2 tsp

Steps:

1. Preheat the oven to 356°F (180°C).
2. In a bowl, mix almond flour, erythritol, and baking powder.
3. In another bowl, beat the egg, add melted butter, and vanilla extract, mixing well.
4. Chop the nuts in a blender or with a knife.
5. Gradually add the dry ingredients to the liquid mixture, stirring until smooth.
6. Form small balls from the dough and place them on a baking sheet lined with parchment paper.
7. Bake the cookies for 10-12 minutes until golden brown.
8. Allow the cookies to cool before serving.

8.13 Chia Pudding

Prep time: 10 minutes
Cook time: 2 hours (chilling)
Nutritional Value: 250 kcal per serving | 20 g fats | 5 g proteins | 8 g carbs | 6 g fiber | 100 mg sodium

Ingredients (for 2 servings):

- Chia seeds – 50 g
- Coconut milk – 200 ml
- Vanilla extract – 1 tsp
- Erythritol – to taste
- Berries (for garnish) – to taste

Steps:

1. In a bowl, mix chia seeds, coconut milk, vanilla extract, and erythritol.
2. Stir well and let it sit for 5-10 minutes for the seeds to start swelling.
3. Stir again and leave in the refrigerator for 2 hours or overnight.
4. Garnish with berries before serving.

8.14 Macarons

Prep time: 30 minutes
Cook time: 18 minutes
Nutritional Value: 350 kcal per serving | 28 g fats | 8 g proteins | 10 g carbs | 4 g fiber | 200 mg sodium

Ingredients (for 2 servings):

For the cookies:
- Almond flour – 100 g
- Erythritol – 100 g
- Egg whites – 2
- Cream of tartar – 1/4 tsp
- Vanilla extract – 1 tsp
- Food coloring (optional) – to taste

For the filling:
- Cream cheese – 50 g
- Butter (soft) – 50 g
- Erythritol (powdered) – 30 g
- Vanilla extract – 1/2 tsp

Steps:

For the cookies:

1. Preheat the oven to 302°F (150°C).
2. In a bowl, beat the egg whites with cream of tartar until soft peaks form.
3. Gradually add erythritol, continuing to beat until stiff peaks form.
4. Add vanilla extract and food coloring, if using.
5. In another bowl, mix almond flour with the remaining erythritol.
6. Gently fold the dry ingredients into the egg whites until well combined.
7. Transfer the mixture to a piping bag and pipe small circles onto a baking sheet lined with parchment paper.
8. Let the macarons sit at room temperature for 30 minutes to form a skin.
9. Bake in the oven for 15-18 minutes until light golden brown.
10. Let the macarons cool completely before removing them from the baking sheet.

For the filling:

1. In a bowl, beat cream cheese, soft butter, powdered erythritol, and vanilla extract until smooth and creamy.
2. Transfer the filling to a piping bag and pipe onto one half of a macaron, then sandwich with the other half.

9. DRINKS

9.1 Coffee with Butter

Prep time: **5 minutes**

Cook time: **5 minutes**

Nutritional Value:
250 kcal per serving | 28 g fats | 0 g proteins | 0 g carbs | 0 g fiber | 50 mg sodium

Ingredients (for 2 servings):

- Freshly brewed coffee – 400 ml
- Butter – 2 tbsp
- Coconut oil – 2 tbsp
- Erythritol (optional) – to taste

Steps:

1. Brew the coffee and pour it into cups.
2. Add 1 tbsp of butter and 1 tbsp of coconut oil to each cup.
3. Stir or blend until smooth.
4. Add erythritol to taste.
5. Serve hot.

9.2 Tea with Lemon

Prep time: **5 minutes**

Cook time: **5 minutes**

Nutritional Value:
10 kcal per serving | 0 g fats | 0 g proteins | 3 g carbs | 0 g fiber | 0 mg sodium

Ingredients (for 2 servings):

- Black or green tea – 400 ml
- Lemon – 1
- Erythritol (optional) – to taste

Steps:

1. Brew the tea and pour it into cups.
2. Squeeze the juice of half a lemon into each cup.
3. Add erythritol to taste.
4. Serve hot.

9.3 Coconut Smoothie

Prep time: 5 minutes
Cook time: 5 minutes
Nutritional Value: 300 kcal per serving | 28 g fats | 2 g proteins | 8 g carbs | 5 g fiber | 50 mg sodium

Ingredients (for 2 servings):

- Coconut milk – 200 ml
- Shredded coconut – 50 g
- Avocado – 1
- Erythritol (optional) – to taste
- Ice (optional)

Steps:

1. In a blender, mix coconut milk, shredded coconut, and avocado until smooth.
2. Add erythritol to taste.
3. Add ice if desired and blend again.
4. Pour the smoothie into glasses and serve immediately.

9.4 Avocado Shake

Prep time: 5 minutes
Cook time: 5 minutes
Nutritional Value: 250 kcal per serving | 22 g fats | 3 g proteins | 6 g carbs | 3 g fiber | 40 mg sodium

Ingredients (for 2 servings):

- Avocado – 1
- Cream (30% fat) – 200 ml
- Water – 100 ml
- Lemon juice – 1 tbsp
- Erythritol (optional) – to taste

Steps:

1. In a blender, mix avocado, cream, water, and lemon juice until smooth.
2. Add erythritol to taste and blend again.
3. Pour the shake into glasses and serve immediately.

9.5 Berry Compote

Prep time: 5 minutes
Cook time: 10 minutes
Nutritional Value: 50 kcal per serving | 0 g fats | 1 g proteins | 10 g carbs | 2 g fiber | 0 mg sodium

Ingredients (for 2 servings):

- Frozen or fresh berries (raspberries, blueberries, strawberries) – 200 g
- Water – 500 ml
- Erythritol – 2 tbsp
- Lemon juice – 1 tbsp

Steps:

1. Bring the water to a boil in a saucepan.
2. Add the berries and simmer for 10 minutes.
3. Add erythritol and lemon juice, and stir.
4. Chill the compote before serving.

9.6 Lemonade with Mint

Prep time: 10 minutes

Cook time: 5 minutes

Nutritional Value:
10 kcal per serving | 0 g fats | 0 g proteins | 3 g carbs | 0 g fiber | 0 mg sodium

Ingredients (for 2 servings):

- Water – 500 ml
- Lemon juice – 100 ml (from 2 lemons)
- Erythritol – 2 tbsp
- Fresh mint – 20 g
- Ice – to taste

Steps:

1. In a large bowl, mix the lemon juice and erythritol until fully dissolved.
2. Add water and finely chopped fresh mint.
3. Stir well and let it sit for 5-10 minutes.
4. Strain the lemonade to remove the mint.
5. Pour into glasses, add ice, and garnish with mint leaves.

9.7 Protein Shake

Prep time: 5 minutes

Cook time: 5 minutes

Nutritional Value:
250 kcal per serving | 15 g fats | 20 g proteins | 6 g carbs | 4 g fiber | 100 mg sodium

Ingredients (for 2 servings):

- Protein powder (sugar-free) – 2 scoops
- Almond milk – 400 ml
- Avocado – 1
- Erythritol – 2 tbsp
- Ice – optional

Steps:

1. Blend protein powder, almond milk, avocado, and erythritol until smooth.
2. Add ice if desired and blend again.
3. Pour into glasses and serve immediately.

9.8 Ginger Tea

Prep time: 5 minutes

Cook time: 5 minutes

Nutritional Value:
15 kcal per serving | 0 g fats | 0 g proteins | 4 g carbs | 0 g fiber | 0 mg sodium

Ingredients (for 2 servings):

- Black or green tea – 400 ml
- Fresh ginger – 20 g
- Lemon – 1
- Erythritol – to taste

Steps:

1. Brew the tea and pour into cups.
2. Slice the ginger thinly and add to the tea.
3. Squeeze the juice of half a lemon into each cup.
4. Add erythritol to taste.
5. Let the tea steep for 5 minutes before serving.

9.9 Nut Milkshake

Prep time: 5 minutes

Cook time: 5 minutes

Nutritional Value: 300 kcal per serving | 25 g fats | 5 g proteins | 8 g carbs | 4 g fiber | 50 mg sodium

Ingredients (for 2 servings):

- Almond milk – 400 ml
- Cream (30% fat) – 100 ml
- Nuts (almonds, walnuts) – 50 g
- Erythritol – 2 tbsp
- Vanilla extract – 1 tsp
- Ice – optional

Steps:

1. Blend almond milk, cream, nuts, erythritol, and vanilla extract until smooth.
2. Add ice if desired and blend again.
3. Pour into glasses and serve immediately.

9.10 Green Smoothie

Prep time: 5 minutes

Cook time: 5 minutes

Nutritional Value: 200 kcal per serving | 18 g fats | 3 g proteins | 6 g carbs | 4 g fiber | 30 mg sodium

Ingredients (for 2 servings):

- Spinach – 100 g
- Avocado – 1
- Almond milk – 200 ml
- Lemon juice – 1 tbsp
- Erythritol – to taste
- Ice – optional

Steps:

1. Blend spinach, avocado, almond milk, and lemon juice until smooth.
2. Add erythritol to taste.
3. Add ice if desired and blend again.
4. Pour into glasses and serve immediately.

9.11 Coconut Milk

Prep time: 5 minutes

Cook time: 5 minutes

Nutritional Value: 150 kcal per serving | 15 g fats | 1 g proteins | 4 g carbs | 2 g fiber | 10 mg sodium

Ingredients (for 2 servings):

- Shredded coconut – 100 g
- Water – 500 ml

Steps:

1. Blend shredded coconut and water until smooth.
2. Strain the mixture through cheesecloth or a fine mesh sieve to separate the liquid from the coconut solids.
3. Pour the coconut milk into a bottle and store in the refrigerator until serving.

9.12 Almond Milk

Prep time: 8 hours (soaking)
Cook time: 10 minutes

Nutritional Value:
100 kcal per serving | 8 g fats | 3 g proteins | 2 g carbs | 1 g fiber | 5 mg sodium

Ingredients (for 2 servings):

- Almonds – 100 g
- Water – 500 ml
- Erythritol (optional) – to taste
- Vanilla extract (optional) – 1/2 tsp

Steps:

1. Soak the almonds in water overnight (or for at least 8 hours).
2. Drain and rinse the almonds.
3. Blend almonds and water until smooth.
4. Strain the mixture through cheesecloth or a fine mesh sieve to separate the liquid from the almond solids.
5. Add erythritol and vanilla extract to taste, if desired.
6. Pour the almond milk into a bottle and store in the refrigerator until serving.

9.13 Hot Chocolate

Prep time: 5 minutes
Cook time: 10 minutes

Nutritional Value:
200 kcal per serving | 18 g fats | 3 g proteins | 6 g carbs | 2 g fiber | 50 mg sodium

Ingredients (for 2 servings):

- Almond milk – 400 ml
- Cocoa powder – 2 tbsp
- Erythritol – 2 tbsp
- Cream (30% fat) – 100 ml
- Vanilla extract – 1/2 tsp

Steps:

1. In a saucepan over medium heat, mix almond milk, cocoa powder, and erythritol.
2. Stir constantly and bring to a boil.
3. Reduce heat and add cream and vanilla extract.
4. Cook for another 2-3 minutes, continuing to stir.
5. Pour the hot chocolate into cups and serve immediately.

9.14 Cinnamon Tea

Prep time: 5 minutes
Cook time: 5 minutes

Nutritional Value:
10 kcal per serving | 0 g fats | 0 g proteins | 3 g carbs | 0 g fiber | 0 mg sodium

Ingredients (for 2 servings):

- Black or green tea – 400 ml
- Cinnamon stick – 1
- Erythritol – to taste
- Lemon – 1/2

Steps:

1. Brew the tea and pour into cups.
2. Add half a cinnamon stick to each cup.
3. Add erythritol to taste.
4. Squeeze the juice of half a lemon into each cup.
5. Let the tea steep for 5 minutes before serving.

Meal Plan for first Week

Day 1

Breakfast: 1.1 Omelet with Avocado and Cheese

Lunch: 2.1 Keto Rolls with Salmon and Avocado

Dinner: 3.1 Baked Beef with Rosemary

Daily Nutritional Value: 1050 kcal | 76 g fats | 75 g proteins | 16 g carbs | 7 g fiber | 800 mg sodium

Day 2

Breakfast: 1.2 Scrambled Eggs with Bacon and Greens

Lunch: 2.2 Keto Salad with Tuna and Egg

Dinner: 3.2 Chicken Breasts in Creamy Sauce

Daily Nutritional Value: 950 kcal | 65 g fats | 60 g proteins | 12 g carbs | 4 g fiber | 600 mg sodium

Day 3

Breakfast: 1.3 Keto Pancakes with Almond Flour

Lunch: 2.3 Keto Cauliflower Soup

Dinner: 3.3 Pork in Keto Barbecue Sauce

Daily Nutritional Value: 900 kcal | 60 g fats | 55 g proteins | 22 g carbs | 8 g fiber | 550 mg sodium

Day 4

Breakfast: 1.4 Keto Waffles with Coconut Flour

Lunch: 2.4 Keto Chicken and Avocado Soup

Dinner: 3.4 Keto Spaghetti with Meat Sauce

Daily Nutritional Value: 950 kcal | 68 g fats | 58 g proteins | 14 g carbs | 5 g fiber | 600 mg sodium

Day 5

Breakfast: 1.5 Keto Chia Seed Porridge

Lunch: 2.5 Keto Chicken and Cheese Sandwich

Dinner: 3.5 Baked Lamb with Garlic and Rosemary

Daily Nutritional Value: 980 kcal | 70 g fats | 63 g proteins | 20 g carbs | 9 g fiber | 650 mg sodium

Day 6

Breakfast: 1.6 Scrambled Eggs with Salmon and Spinach

Lunch: 2.6 Keto Cupcakes with Bacon and Cheese

Dinner: 3.6 Fried Duck with Orange Sauce

Daily Nutritional Value: 1050 kcal | 75 g fats | 70 g proteins | 18 g carbs | 6 g fiber | 800 mg sodium

Day 7

Breakfast: 1.7 Avocado Baked with Egg

Lunch: 2.7 Keto Zucchini Fritters

Dinner: 3.7 Chicken Curry with Coconut Milk

Daily Nutritional Value: 920 kcal | 68 g fats | 55 g proteins | 15 g carbs | 6 g fiber | 700 mg sodium

Meal Plan for second Week

Day 8

Breakfast: 1.8 Keto Avocado Cocoa Pudding

Lunch: 2.8 Caprese Salad with Avocado

Dinner: 3.8 Ribs Baked with Garlic and Rosemary

Daily Nutritional Value: 1000 kcal | 75 g fats | 55 g proteins | 20 g carbs | 10 g fiber | 700 mg sodium

Day 9

Breakfast: 1.9 Keto Pancakes with Berries

Lunch: 2.9 Keto Cheese Sticks

Dinner: 3.9 Beef with Mushrooms in Cream Sauce

Daily Nutritional Value: 1050 kcal | 78 g fats | 63 g proteins | 20 g carbs | 7 g fiber | 750 mg sodium

Day 10

Breakfast: 1.10 Frittata with Vegetables and Cheese

Lunch: 2.10 Keto Tacos with Lettuce Leaves

Dinner: 3.10 Baked Turkey with Brussels Sprouts

Daily Nutritional Value: 980 kcal | 70 g fats | 65 g proteins | 15 g carbs | 8 g fiber | 650 mg sodium

Day 11

Breakfast: 1.11 Shakshuka with Sausages

Lunch: 2.11 Keto Omelet Roll with Vegetables

Dinner: 3.11 Chicken Skewers with Green Vegetables

Daily Nutritional Value: 1020 kcal | 75 g fats | 70 g proteins | 18 g carbs | 6 g fiber | 700 mg sodium

Day 12

Breakfast: 1.12 Keto Granola with Coconut and Nuts

Lunch: 2.12 Keto Mushroom Cream Soup

Dinner: 3.12 Beef Roll with Spinach and Cheese Filling

Daily Nutritional Value: 1050 kcal | 80 g fats | 60 g proteins | 15 g carbs | 7 g fiber | 750 mg sodium

Day 13

Breakfast: 1.13 Salad with Eggs and Avocado

Lunch: 2.13 Keto Burgers on Lettuce Leaves

Dinner: 3.13 Spiced Pork Roast

Daily Nutritional Value: 1000 kcal | 75 g fats | 65 g proteins | 12 g carbs | 6 g fiber | 700 mg sodium

Day 14

Breakfast: 1.14 Keto Smoothie with Spinach and Avocado

Lunch: 2.14 Keto Bruschetta with Tomatoes and Basil

Dinner: 3.14 Keto Chicken and Avocado Burger

Daily Nutritional Value: 950 kcal | 70 g fats | 58 g proteins | 15 g carbs | 7 g fiber | 600 mg sodium

Meal Plan for third Week

Day 15

Breakfast: 1.1 Omelet with Avocado and Cheese

Lunch: 4.1 Cauliflower "Rice"

Dinner: 5.1 Keto Mayonnaise with Baked Chicken

Daily Nutritional Value: 950 kcal | 70 g fats | 55 g proteins | 14 g carbs | 5 g fiber | 650 mg sodium

Day 16

Breakfast: 1.2 Scrambled Eggs with Bacon and Greens

Lunch: 4.2 Zucchini Noodles with Garlic

Dinner: 5.2 Keto Caesar Sauce with Chicken Salad

Daily Nutritional Value: 900 kcal | 65 g fats | 55 g proteins | 12 g carbs | 4 g fiber | 600 mg sodium

Day 17

Breakfast: 1.3 Keto Pancakes with Almond Flour

Lunch: 4.3 Keto Almond Flour Bread with Avocado

Dinner: 5.3 Keto Pesto with Chicken Breasts

Daily Nutritional Value: 980 kcal | 70 g fats | 60 g proteins | 18 g carbs | 7 g fiber | 650 mg sodium

Day 18

Breakfast: 1.4 Keto Waffles with Coconut Flour

Lunch: 4.4 Cauliflower Mash with Fried Fish

Dinner: 5.4 Creamy Garlic Sauce with Chicken Fillet

Daily Nutritional Value: 960 kcal | 68 g fats | 58 g proteins | 14 g carbs | 5 g fiber | 600 mg sodium

Day 19

Breakfast: 1.5 Keto Chia Seed Porridge

Lunch: 4.5 Baked Brussels Sprouts with Chicken

Dinner: 5.5 Guacamole Sauce with Fried Beef

Daily Nutritional Value: 950 kcal | 70 g fats | 58 g proteins | 18 g carbs | 6 g fiber | 650 mg sodium

Day 20

Breakfast: 1.6 Scrambled Eggs with Salmon and Spinach

Lunch: 4.6 Grilled Mushrooms with Chicken Wings

Dinner: 5.6 Keto Garlic Sauce with Baked Lamb

Daily Nutritional Value: 1050 kcal | 75 g fats | 65 g proteins | 14 g carbs | 6 g fiber | 700 mg sodium

Day 21

Breakfast: 1.7 Avocado Baked with Egg

Lunch: 4.7 Spinach and Nuts Salad with Chicken Patties

Dinner: 5.7 Keto Tartar Sauce with Fried Fish

Daily Nutritional Value: 980 kcal | 70 g fats | 60 g proteins | 15 g carbs | 5 g fiber | 650 mg sodium

Meal Plan for fourth Week

Day 22

Breakfast: 1.8 Keto Avocado Cocoa Pudding

Lunch: 4.8 Grilled Eggplant with Garlic and Chicken Fillet

Dinner: 5.8 Keto Alfredo Sauce with Chicken Breasts

Daily Nutritional Value: 950 kcal | 70 g fats | 58 g proteins | 14 g carbs | 6 g fiber | 600 mg sodium

Day 23

Breakfast: 1.9 Keto Pancakes with Berries

Lunch: 4.9 Keto "Potato" with Radish and Fried Fish

Dinner: 5.9 Keto Barbecue Sauce with Ribs

Daily Nutritional Value: 1000 kcal | 75 g fats | 65 g proteins | 18 g carbs | 7 g fiber | 650 mg sodium

Day 24

Breakfast: 1.10 Frittata with Vegetables and Cheese

Lunch: 4.10 Green Beans with Bacon and Chicken Fillet

Dinner: 5.10 Keto Marinara Sauce with Meatballs

Daily Nutritional Value: 980 kcal | 70 g fats | 60 g proteins | 16 g carbs | 5 g fiber | 600 mg sodium

Day 25

Breakfast: 1.11 Shakshuka with Sausages

Lunch: 4.11 Fried Zucchini with Cheese and Chicken Fillet

Dinner: 5.11 Keto Hollandaise Sauce with Fried Fish

Daily Nutritional Value: 1050 kcal | 78 g fats | 65 g proteins | 14 g carbs | 6 g fiber | 700 mg sodium

Day 26

Breakfast: 1.12 Keto Granola with Coconut and Nuts

Lunch: 4.12 Keto Flaxseed Crackers with Avocado

Dinner: 5.12 Keto Ranch Sauce with Baked Chicken

Daily Nutritional Value: 950 kcal | 70 g fats | 58 g proteins | 18 g carbs | 8 g fiber | 650 mg sodium

Day 27

Breakfast: 1.13 Salad with Eggs and Avocado

Lunch: 4.13 Cabbage Salad with Avocado and Chicken Fillet

Dinner: 5.13 Salsa Sauce with Fried Beef

Daily Nutritional Value: 980 kcal | 72 g fats | 60 g proteins | 14 g carbs | 6 g fiber | 600 mg sodium

Day 28

Breakfast: 1.14 Keto Smoothie with Spinach and Avocado

Lunch: 4.14 Baked Sweet Pepper with Chicken Fillet

Dinner: 5.14 Keto Cream Cheese Sauce with Baked Fish

Daily Nutritional Value: 950 kcal | 70 g fats | 58 g proteins | 15 g carbs | 7 g fiber | 650 mg sodium

GROCERY LIST for Week 1

Meat and Fish

Salmon – 2 lbs

Chicken Breasts – 2.6 lbs

Beef – 2.4 lbs

Pork – 1.75 lbs

Turkey Fillet – 0.65 lbs

Chicken Wings – 1.1 lbs

Fish (choice for baking) – 0.65 lbs

Vegetables and Greens

Avocados – 5

Cucumber – 2

Zucchini – 1

Green Pepper – 1

Onion – 3

Garlic – 10 cloves

Red Onion – 1

Spinach (fresh) – 7 oz

Carrot – 1

Broccoli – 14 oz

Cauliflower – 1

Brussels Sprouts – 7 oz

Lettuce Leaves – 6

Tomatoes – 3

Cherry Tomatoes – 7 oz

Asparagus – 7 oz

Parsley (fresh) – 1 bunch

Cilantro (fresh) – 1 bunch

Rosemary – 1 bunch

Thyme – 1 bunch

Fruits and Berries

Lemon – 4

Berries (choice) – 7 oz

Orange – 1

Dairy Products

Butter – 10.5 oz

Heavy Cream (30% fat) – 2.5 cups

Cheese (Cheddar or Mozzarella) – 14 oz

Cream Cheese – 1.75 oz

Coconut Milk – 7 fl oz

Nuts and Seeds

Almond Flour – 7 oz

Chia Seeds – 3.5 oz

Nuts (choice for granola) – 7 oz

Fats and Oils

Olive Oil – 1.7 cups

Coconut Oil – 1.75 oz

Sauces

Soy Sauce (sugar-free) – 3.5 fl oz

Spices and Seasonings

Paprika – 1 tsp

Red Pepper (ground) – 1 tsp

Mustard – 2 tbsp

Curry Paste – 2 tbsp

GROCERY LIST for Week 2

Meat and Fish

Chicken Breasts – 3.3 lbs

Salmon – 1.3 lbs

Beef – 1.3 lbs

Pork – 1.1 lbs

Turkey – 0.65 lbs

Fish Fillet – 0.65 lbs

Chicken Thighs – 0.65 lbs

Vegetables and Greens

Avocados – 6

Cucumber – 1

Cherry Tomatoes – 7 oz

Onion – 4

Red Onion – 1

Spinach (fresh) – 7 oz

Carrot – 1

Broccoli – 7 oz

Cauliflower – 1

Brussels Sprouts – 7 oz

Lettuce Leaves – 6

Tomatoes – 3

Asparagus – 7 oz

Zucchini – 1

Green Pepper – 1

Eggplant – 1

Parsley (fresh) – 1 bunch

Cilantro (fresh) – 1 bunch

Rosemary – 1 bunch

Thyme – 1 bunch

Fresh Basil – 1 bunch

Fruits and Berries

Lemon – 5

Berries (choice) – 7 oz

Dairy Products

Butter – 10.5 oz

Heavy Cream (30% fat) – 2.5 cups

Cheese (Cheddar or Mozzarella) – 14 oz

Cream Cheese – 1.75 oz

Coconut Milk – 7 fl oz

Nuts and Seeds

Almond Flour – 7 oz

Chia Seeds – 3.5 oz

Nuts (choice for granola) – 7 oz

Fats and Oils

Olive Oil – 1.7 cups

Coconut Oil – 1.75 oz

Sauces

Soy Sauce (sugar-free) – 3.5 fl oz

Spices and Seasonings

Paprika – 1 tsp

Red Pepper (ground) – 1 tsp

Mustard – 2 tbsp

Curry Paste – 2 tbsp

Bay Leaf – 1 pack

GROCERY LIST for Week 3

Meat and Fish

Chicken Breasts – 2.6 lbs

Beef – 2 lbs

Pork – 1.1 lbs

Turkey – 0.65 lbs

Salmon – 0.65 lbs

Chicken Wings – 1.1 lbs

Fish Fillet – 0.65 lbs

Vegetables and Greens

Avocados – 6

Cucumber – 2

Zucchini – 1

Green Pepper – 1

Onion – 4

Garlic – 10 cloves

Red Onion – 1

Spinach (fresh) – 7 oz

Carrot – 1

Broccoli – 7 oz

Cauliflower – 1

Brussels Sprouts – 7 oz

Lettuce Leaves – 6

Tomatoes – 3

Cherry Tomatoes – 7 oz

Asparagus – 7 oz

Mushrooms – 7 oz

Parsley (fresh) – 1 bunch

Cilantro (fresh) – 1 bunch

Rosemary – 1 bunch

Thyme – 1 bunch

Fruits and Berries

Lemon – 5

Berries (choice) – 7 oz

Dairy Products

Butter – 10.5 oz

Heavy Cream (30% fat) – 2.5 cups

Cheese (Cheddar or Mozzarella) – 14 oz

Cream Cheese – 1.75 oz

Coconut Milk – 7 fl oz

Nuts and Seeds

Almond Flour – 7 oz

Chia Seeds – 3.5 oz

Nuts (choice for granola) – 7 oz

Fats and Oils

Olive Oil – 1.7 cups

Coconut Oil – 1.75 oz

Sauces

Soy Sauce (sugar-free) – 3.5 fl oz

Spices and Seasonings

Paprika – 1 tsp

Red Pepper (ground) – 1 tsp

Mustard – 2 tbsp

Curry Paste – 2 tbsp

Bay Leaf – 1 pack

GROCERY LIST for Week 4

Meat and Fish

Chicken Breasts – 2.6 lbs

Beef – 1.3 lbs

Pork – 1.1 lbs

Turkey – 0.65 lbs

Salmon – 0.65 lbs

Chicken Thighs – 0.65 lbs

Fish Fillet – 0.65 lbs

Vegetables and Greens

Avocados – 6

Cucumber – 1

Zucchini – 1

Green Pepper – 1

Onion – 4

Garlic – 10 cloves

Red Onion – 1

Spinach (fresh) – 7 oz

Carrot – 1

Broccoli – 7 oz

Cauliflower – 1

Brussels Sprouts – 7 oz

Lettuce Leaves – 6

Tomatoes – 3

Cherry Tomatoes – 7 oz

Asparagus – 7 oz

Mushrooms – 7 oz

Parsley (fresh) – 1 bunch

Cilantro (fresh) – 1 bunch

Rosemary – 1 bunch

Thyme – 1 bunch

Eggplant – 1

Sweet Pepper – 2

Fruits and Berries

Lemon – 5

Berries (choice) – 7 oz

Dairy Products

Butter – 10.5 oz

Heavy Cream (30% fat) – 2.5 cups

Cheese (Cheddar or Mozzarella) – 14 oz

Cream Cheese – 1.75 oz

Coconut Milk – 7 fl oz

Nuts and Seeds

Almond Flour – 7 oz

Chia Seeds – 3.5 oz

Nuts (choice for granola) – 7 oz

Fats and Oils

Olive Oil – 1.7 cups

Coconut Oil – 1.75 oz

Sauces

Soy Sauce (sugar-free) – 3.5 fl oz

Spices and Seasonings

Paprika – 1 tsp

Red Pepper (ground) – 1 tsp

Mustard – 2 tbsp

Curry Paste – 2 tbsp

Bay Leaf – 1 pack

Reference page

Brinkworth, Grant D., Manny Noakes, Jonathan D. Buckley, Jennifer B. Keogh, and Peter M. Clifton. "Long-Term Effects of a Very-Low-Carbohydrate Weight Loss Diet Compared with an Isocaloric Low-Fat Diet after 12 Mo." The American Journal of Clinical Nutrition 90, no. 1 (July 2009): 23-32. doi:10.3945 /ajen.2008.27326.

Allen, Bryan G., Sudershan K. Bhatia, Carryn M. Anderson, Julie M.

Eichenberger-Gilmore, et al. "Ketogenic Diets as an Adjuvant Cancer Therapy:

History and Potential Mechanism." Redox Biology vol. 2 (2014): 963-70.

doi:10.1016/j.redox.2014.08.002

Aude, Y., A. S., Agatston, F. Lopez-Jimenez, et al. "The National Cholesterol Education Program Diet vs a Diet Lower in Carbohydrates and Higher in Protein and Monounsaturated Fat: A Randomized Trial." JAMA Internal Medicine 164, no. 19 (2004): 2141-46. doi: 10.1001/archinte.164.19.2141.

Brehm, Bonnie J., Randy J. Seeley, Stephen R. Daniels, and David A. D'Alessio.

"A Randomized Trial Comparing a Very Low Carbohydrate Diet and a Calorie-Restricted Low Fat Diet on Body Weight and Cardiovascular Risk Factors in Healthy Women." The Journal of Clinical Endocrinology & Metabolism 88, no. 4 (January 2009). doi: 10.1210/jc.2002-021480.

Chowdhury, R., S. Warnakula, S. Kunutsor, F. Crowe, H. A. Ward, et al.

"Association of Dietary, Circulating, and Supplement Fatty Acids with Coronary Risk: A Systematic Review and Meta-Analysis." Annals of Internal Medicine 160 (2014): 398-406. doi:10.7326/M13-1788.

Paoli, Antonio, Antonino Bianco, Ernesto Damiani, and Gerardo Basco. "Ketogenic Diet in Neuromuscular and Neurodegenerative Diseases." Biomed Research International 474296 (2014). doi:10.1155/2014/474296.

Samaha, Frederick F., Nayyar Iqbal, Prakash Seshadri, Kathryn L. Chicano, et al.

"A Low-Carbohydrate as Compared with a Low-Fat Diet in Severe Obesity." The New England Journal of Medicine 348 (May 2003): 2075-81. doi:10.1056

/NEJMoao22637.

Siri-Tarino, P. W., Q. Sun, F. B. Hu, and R. M. Krauss. "Meta-Analysis of Prospective Cohort Studies Evaluating the Association of Saturated Fat with Cardiovascular Disease." American Journal of Clinical Nutrition 91, no. 3 (March 2010): 535-46. doi:10.3945/ajcn.2009.27/25.

Sondike, Stephen B., Nancy Copperman, and Marc S. Jacobson. "Effects of a Low-Carbohydrate Diet on Weight Loss and Cardiovascular Risk Factor in Overweight Adolescents." The Journal of Pediatrics 142, no. 3 (March 2003): 253-58. doi: 10.1067/mpd.2003.4-"Statistics About Diabetes." American Diabetes Association. www.diabetes.org

/diabetes-basics/statistics/.

Tetzloff, W., F. Dauchy, S. Medimagh, D. Carr, A. Bärr. "Tolerance to Subchronic, High-Dose Ingestion of Erythritol in Human Volunteers." Regulatory Toxicology and Pharmacology 24, no, 2 (October 1996): S286-95. doi:10.1006 /rtph.1996.010.

Vanitallie, T. B., C. Nonas, A. Di Rocco, K. Boyar, S. B. Heymshield. "Treatment of Parkinson Disease with Diet-Induced Hyperketonemia: A Feasibility Study." Neurology 64, no. 4 (February 2005): 728-30. doi:10.1212 /01. WNL.0000152046.11390.45.

Volek, J. S., S. D. Phinney, C. E. Forsythe, et al. "Carbohydrate Restriction Has a More Favorable Impact on the Metabolic Syndrome than a Low Fat Diet." Lipids 44, no. 4 (2009): 297. doi:10.1007/511745-008-3274-2.

Daly, M. E., R. Paisey, R. Paisey, B. A. Millward, et al. "Short-Term Effects of Severe Dietary Carbohydrate-Restriction Advice in Type 2 Diabetes-a Randomized Controlled Trial." Diabetic Medicine 23, no. 1 (January 2006):

15-20. doi:10.1111/j.1464-5491.2005.01760.x.

Davis, C., and E. Saltos. "Dietary Recommendations and How They Have

Changed Over Time," Agriculture Information Bulletin No. (AIB-750) 494 PP, U.S. Department of Agriculture, May 1999: 36-44. www.ers.usda.gov //media/91022/aib750b_1_pdf.

Freeman, J. M., E. P. Vining, D. J. Pillas, P. L. Pyzik, et al. "The Efficacy of the Ketogenic Diet-1998: A Prospective Evaluation of Intervention in 150 Children." Pediatrics 102, no. 6 (December 1998): 1358-63. www.ncbi.nlm.nih.gov /pubmed/9832569/.

Fryar, C. D., M. D. Carroll, and C. L. Ogden. "Prevalence of Overweight, Obesity, and Extreme Obesity Among Adults: United States, 1960-1962 Through

2011-2012." Centers for Disease Control and Prevention, September 2014.

www.cdc.gov/nchs/data/hestat/obesity_adult_11_12/obesity_adult_11_12

htm#table2.

Hemingway, C., J. M. Freeman, D. J. Pillas, and P. L. Pyzik. "The Ketogenic Diet:

A 3to 6-Year Follow-Up of 150 Children Enrolled Prospectively. Pediatrics 108, no. 4 (October 2001): 898-905. www.ncbi.nlm.nih.gov/pubmed/11581442/ Henderson, S. T. "High Carbohydrate Diets and Alzheimer's Disease." Medical Hypotheses 62, no. 5 (2014): 68g-700. doi:10.1016/j.mehy.2003.11.028.

Neal, E. G., H. Chaffe, R. H. Schwartz, M. S. Lawson, et al. "The Ketogenic Diet for the Treatment of Childhood Epilepsy: A Randomised Controlled Trial." Lancet Neurology 7, no. 6 (June 2008): 500-06. doi: 10.1016/51474-4422(08)70092-9

Otto, C., U. Kaemmerer, B. Illert, B. Muehling, et al. "Growth of Human Gastric Cancer Cells in Nude Mice Is Delayed by a Ketogenic Diet Supplemented with Omega-3 Fatty Acids and Medium-Chain Triglycerides." BMC

Cancer 8 (April 2008): 122. doi:10.1186/1471-2407-8-122.

Made in the USA
Columbia, SC
17 June 2025